P R A I S E

GORILLA IN THE ROOM

AND OTHER STORIES

"Unlike anything else you'll ever read: warm, funny, often profound, and above all, a celebration of life."

—NEIL HANSON, Author of *Unknown Soldiers*

"The creativity and optimism Ed Tracy brought to his diagnosis underscores this most human story of one man and his journey. *Gorilla in the Room* will delight readers with a mix of theater dialogue, song titles, and stories that entertain and inform. Ed Tracy adeptly guides us through his personal reflection and physical suffering and the lessons to be learned from cancer."

—ELIZABETH M. NORMAN PHD, RN, Author of *We Band of Angels: The Untold Story of American Women Captured on Bataan by the Japanese*

"I love it! . . . The organization into short, evocative chapters, is creative and unique."

—H. R. MCMASTER, Author of *Battlegrounds: The Fight to Defend the Free World*

"With the homespun warmth of *A Prairie Home Companion* and the fantastical framing of a Broadway musical, *Gorilla in the Room and Other Stories* is a remarkable chronicling of one man's resilience and determination when confronted with the diagnosis no one wants to hear. Weaving together a life's journey from farm to fame, a master storyteller and humanist reminds us all of why life is worth fighting for."

—HENRY D. GODINEZ, Professor, Department of Theatre, Northwestern University

"Ed Tracy has created a beautiful artistic approach to his cancer journey. Through essays, letters, and a clever musical script, he takes the reader with him through several relationships and events that molded him and the challenges that cancer brought to his table. Sometimes it can be quite difficult to vocalize the hardship and lessons of illness and of facing your mortality. Theatre has always been a way of reaching the masses in a communal setting and leading them through sometimes joyous but possibly very difficult themes. These 'theatrical' moments in *Gorilla in the Room* do just that. In between lovely, honest essays about his life growing up in Vermont, some very special friendships, and the discovery of his illness, Mr. Tracy has written a musical script that reaches a hand out to the reader, saying, 'Come on this journey with me. Your attendance enriches my journey and hopefully yours as well.' The combination of all of these genres of storytelling swept me up and gave me a seat at the table."

—HEIDI KETTENRING, Actor and Singer

"Ed Tracy offers a unique collection of recollections made vivid by a life changed by the presence of cancer. The metaphors abound, including the 'club' of those touched by cancer. The characters abound, including some individuals you probably know of yourself. The forms abound, including the first cancer musical you have ever encountered. There is an intensity to conversations, letters, and emails that were exchanged with the awareness that each might be the last. Whether you are in the club or not, Ed Tracy's special mode of storytelling will grip you."

—GARY T. JOHNSON, President Emeritus, Chicago History Museum

"Ed Tracy tells a poignant and inspiring story about dealing with, and healing from, cancer. Extremely moving and insightful. A must-read for anyone dealing with adversity."

—DIXIE DAVIS, Author of *Endless Love and Second Chances*

"Ed Tracy faced his cancer journey the same way he has approached life in general: straight-on and with a never-ending passion to determine what adventure comes next. He's made a million friends along the way and collected a billion stories to tell, in addition to accumulating some sage advice that the rest of us would do well to take. *Gorilla in the Room* is a great read from start to finish and reminds us that life is best lived one day at a time, with no assumption of tomorrow."

> **—DAVE MOODY**, Host of Sirius XM Speedway, Sirius XM
> NASCAR Radio, @DGodfatherMoody

"Amazed at your story. As we say in West Virginia—*YOU DONE IT GOOD!*"

> **—HERSHEL "WOODY" WILLIAMS**, World War II Medal of Honor
> Recipient, Iwo Jima

"A touchstone memoir. Japanese writer Haruki Murakami wrote, 'There are some things we can never assign to oblivion, memories we can never rub away. They remain with us forever, like a touchstone.' Ed Tracy's *Gorilla in the Room* toggles among memories as diverse as chemotherapy sessions, fly-fishing in Labrador, writing a musical about Buster Keaton, involvement in theater arts in a New England college, and growing up on a family farm in Vermont. A parade of unique and memorable influencers in cameo roles cross Tracy's life stage, from William Colby and Robert Goulet to Werner Klemperer, Colonel Klink of *Hogan's Heroes*. Longtime mentors and the author's wife, Denise, make frequent and important appearances in these perceptive and moving recollections. It is as if we spent time with author Tracy on a back porch during a New England summer evening, experiencing a gifted storyteller recount, to use his own words, how 'the experiences all summed lead us to a wonderful memory.' This is a substantial compilation of memories artfully presented and well worth reading."

> **—ROBERT C. PLUMB**, Author of *Your Brother in Arms: A Union
> Soldier's Odyssey* and *The Better Angels: Five Women Who
> Changed Civil War America*

"*Gorilla in the Room and Other Stories* is a profound piece of prose by Ed Tracy. As a reader with family members in 'the Club,' Ed's personal story particularly resonated with me and helped make sense of the challenges unique to each cancer patient's journey. Ed's beautifully written reflections on key players in his journey leap off the page—and into the reader's heart—as he evokes visceral responses through a series of captivating vignettes, each offering incredible poignancy and inspiring empathy, and connected by the common element of our shared, flawed, wonderful humanity. As Ed writes, 'Our challenge always is to keep people focused forward, learning and enjoying life, and taking a moment to thank those who show us so much love, even when they might not be in the room.' With this beautiful memoir, Ed has accomplished all that, and so much more."

—KAYLA BOYE, Actor and Arts Administrator

"In his well-crafted memoir, *Gorilla in the Room and Other Stories*, Ed Tracy turns his challenging cancer crusade from an urban chemotherapy ward to the crystal blue waters of Umiakovik Lake into a fascinating series of adventures. Those of us who saw it all happening in real time can attest to the grit, fortitude and humor of a gifted storyteller who tells it like it is, right down to surviving Shakespeare's most famous stage direction: 'Exit, pursued by a bear.'"

—BARRY MEINERTH, Norwich University Class of 1968

"Ed Tracy's memoir evokes a number of adjectives: illuminating, inspirational, and emotionally touching. The series of tales is reminiscent of Forrest Gump's fabled box of chocolates as a metaphor for life: you never know what you're going to get. These stories, like chocolates, are highly addictive."

—PAUL STILLWELL, Historian and Author

"Ed Tracy's *Gorilla in the Room and Other Stories* reflects upon the personal validation of life when forced into focus by those of us in jeopardy of losing it. Ed's approach is unique in that it blends theatrical script with personal autobiographical missives. Acts revealing the common uncertainty realized by all 'the Club's' heterogeneous membership and chapters of autobiographical records bringing to fore the emotional fullness of life's endeavors. The depth of personal introspection of those faced with chemotherapy could only be told by Ed looking into his own soul's history. 'The long-term prognosis was simple and vague: three years, thumbs-up; five years, pop the champagne!'"

—YANK SHUGG, Norwich University Class of 1968

"A must-read. Anecdotal recollections take you through a compelling lifetime journey of personal memories, as well as observations about personalities from Chicago luminaries through national theatrical figures and American heroes, all the narrative being interwoven with a theater script focusing on fighting cancer—the gorilla lurking in the background."

—JOHN ZUKOWSKY, Chicago Author and Retired Museum Professional

GORILLA IN THE ROOM

AND OTHER STORIES

ED TRACY

Foreword by FRANK SESNO

VIRGINIA BEACH
CAPE CHARLES

*Gorilla in the Room
and Other Stories*

by Ed Tracy

© Copyright 2020 Ed Tracy

ISBN 978-1-64663-305-0

Cover art by James Dietz

Published by

◤ köehlerbooks™

3705 Shore Drive
Virginia Beach, VA 23455
800-435-4811
www.koehlerbooks.com

To members of "the Club"

and to their loved ones

whose unwavering courage

is an example for us all.

FOREWORD

AS A JOURNALIST, I have had the great privilege in life of sitting in the front row of history, covering presidents and politics, global crises and dramatic breakthroughs. I have had the opportunity to meet and interview amazing people—more than I can count—posing questions to get explanation and insight, clarity and candor. I am fascinated by people and their stories. I gravitate toward those who are active and curious, who ask piercing questions, who can help me learn and discover, who are storytellers.

Ed Tracy is one of those people, and he does all those things in this book. He has written a moving testament to life, resilience, creativity, and iron determination.

I met Ed in 1998 at Norwich University in Northfield, Vermont. He'd invited me to moderate a conversation on "Ethics in Military Literature and Film" at the William E. Colby Military Writers' Symposium. I was an anchor at CNN, and Ed wanted me to engage some of the leading military authors of our time. Ed showed me around the campus and proudly introduced me to the students. The event was packed and drew local media. Ed was in his element, reveling in the exchange of ideas and deep discussion among compelling people who had both made and chronicled history.

Little did any of us know that Ed would later help launch a major military library and produce some of the most meaningful dialogues of our time. Little did Ed know that cancer would intrude and threaten to derail his dream and cut short his life.

This book traces Ed's journey—from his hometown in rural Vermont to New York and, later, Chicago, where he launched a military conversation series and became a theater critic. We travel with and learn from him as his worlds collide when his doctors tell him he has stage 3 colon cancer. Confronted with wrenching decisions and his own mortality, he pushes himself through a medical maze, chemotherapy, and physical and emotional exhaustion.

Woven with insight, candor, and humor, *Gorilla in the Room and Other Stories* takes us on a unique backstage journey to peer through cancer's thick curtain. We applaud as we watch Ed navigate the uncertainty, dread, and soaring hope that accompany this experience. He looks ahead with hope. He flashes back for perspective. A letter of love to his daughter, Amanda. Conversations with his classmates. Revelations and reunions. During one, a confrontation with the darkest family secret—his mother's alcoholism.

Ed introduces us to a rich and varied cast of characters in his life—authors and military heroes, professors and thinkers, common folk, family, and his very funny rock of a wife, Denise. Others drop in through the musical that plays on in a parallel universe of cancer and comedy. Meet Joe Gorilla, Tess and Toss Terone and the Chaosals. Absurd? Profound? People come into our lives for a reason, Ed explains. And they all have a story to tell.

Gorilla in the Room and Other Stories invites you into the lifechanging "club" of those who have had cancer. For those who belong to that club, this engaging and reflective book will serve as a GPS for the uneven and perilous road traveled. For others, the book will inspire you to treasure the people, places, and precious gift of time we too often take for granted.

Facing the unexpected and the existential, Ed Tracy writes with a critical eye and a special clarity. Theater is both his love—and his metaphor. "Challenge the audience," he tells us. "Get in their face. Be loud and boisterous."

Words to live by.

Frank Sesno
Professor of Media and Public Affairs
George Washington University
Author of *Ask More*
October 4, 2020

PROLOGUE

BACK IN 2008, I did not use social media or a care page to explore my cancer journey. I attribute that choice to Rule No. 4—you'll see that the path I am on has led to a lot of rules—and a perceived need to focus on my work when I felt well, and not to be burdened by a massive amount of tell-all commentary when I did not. One of the symptoms of my particular treatment made accurate typing difficult. So, just the thought of responding to anyone via email was stressful. Rather than writing anything down, I recorded audio notes to myself. And, as an ever-widening group of friends and associates learned about my situation, I continued to write a journal, of sorts, that I thought might someday become an important, and even helpful, essay for members of "the Club" and others who were interested.

Somewhere along the way, other ideas began to emerge in my memory. Stories about people I knew. Essays based on an actual event or a series of events. Then a few individual conversations merged into one—vivid recollections of firsthand experiences I had, either alone or with a few other people who I came to realize had, in the process, made a profound impact on my life.

The following is the result of that work, edited from time to time over the years. I have not named names, unless it is obvious, in what has become a personal story of my cancer journey. Beloved pets and great works of fiction wait for another day.

My aim in this is to let you know what I have discovered and how it has changed my life. I hope this might be helpful to those dealing with cancer in their lives, inspiring to all members of "the Club," and a rallying call to those who have, for whatever reason, delayed getting testing and treatment.

The walk we are on starts with one positive step.

This was mine.

JUNE 30, 2020

TABLE OF CONTENTS

Act I, Scene 1

This is the Club we're in
there's no invitation
Because the Club we're in
doesn't really care
This is the Club we're in
got one consolation
This is the Club we're in
for the rest of our lives.

Ensemble
Act 1, Scene 1

CHAPTER 1

ACT I, SCENE 1

SETTING: Exterior Office Building and City Street. Present.

NOTE: The pre-show announcement includes the statement "(Insert number) of the cast members, crew, and creative team in tonight's production of GORILLA IN THE ROOM have faced or are facing cancer as a patient, survivor, caregiver, or family member. This production is presented in honor of their unwavering courage."

SONGS: THE CLUB (WE'RE IN)

AT RISE: A brief, spirited, upbeat overture leads to the GORILLA IN THE ROOM theme.

A brisk fall day begins outside a 1930s-era office building; streetlamps flicker to reveal an urban street location. The building has a large central arch with the words "TREATMENT CENTER" over the revolving door.

One by one, the ENSEMBLE creates business on the street: an anxious couple hailing a cab, a woman with a stroller, executives engaged in conversation, and service employees.

DR. THOMPSON appears in the crowd and proceeds through the building's revolving door. The GORILLA IN THE ROOM theme transforms into THE CLUB (WE'RE IN).

Enter KATHARINE, SAM and JACK. KATHARINE sings. Her father joins her, and successively the ENSEMBLE arrives at the treatment center throughout the number.

As all enter through the revolving door, the walls of the building separate to reveal the center lobby and elevator.

TESS and TOSS TERONE wait at the elevator, which is imaginatively framed and isolated center stage. MOTHER joins them.

As the elevator appears to rise one floor, COLIN and family, along with BAKER and BROWN, step in. When the elevator appears to rise to the third floor, the doors open, and all enter the treatment center's waiting room, which has settled into position on stage left and stage right. The elevator rotates from upstage to downstage on an axis. THE CLUB (WE'RE IN) culminates in a full-COMPANY number in the waiting-room area.

CHAPTER 2

DEFINING MOMENTS

I REMEMBER TWO MOMENTS about the day in particular.

There was a moment when the door opened and I thought there would be good news. I had completed nine laps around the unit in the morning, and I wanted to get out and back home a few days ahead of schedule. And I had made it back and forth to the john on my own, despite a foot-long incision after being opened up like a tuna a few days before.

Denise, my longtime soul mate, and I had been scheduled to meet with my surgeon an hour earlier, so he immediately apologized for being late. He explained that he had wanted to be sure he had everything in order before we talked.

He apologized again for being overly optimistic in advance of the surgery by putting the chances of any further treatment so low.

There will be more, he said.

It will be necessary.

And aggressive.

So, in that second moment, I realized my life had changed drastically, and that I would have to become a very active listener.

For in that second moment, I could not think of a thing to say.

CHAPTER 3

DEAR JOHN—HUNTING

Dear John,

I have been thinking a lot recently about hunting.

There is a certain rite of passage between a father and his sons. It doesn't matter how old the sons are. It only matters that there are men in the room who want to relate to each other and to those around them in a basic way: proving to each other that they have somehow achieved a certain level of understanding and accomplishment.

Hunting season in my family was a ritual. Unless there were some animals intruding on our property, or a guest asked to see them, I do not recall the rifles that my father stored on a shelf high out of reach over our cellar stairway ever coming out of their place except for in the days leading up to hunting season. Then, almost casually, my father brought them outside, opened the chamber, and carefully held the barrel toward the light to see if any dust had accumulated over the previous year. He would cut the corner off a rag, oil it, and jam it down the shaft of the gun, and then rummage through a drawer in the cellar until he found the box of .30-30 shells he had purchased decades before.

So, you could say that hunting was a pastime in our family, but we did little of the shooting part. My father hunted deer for necessity, not for sport. Unlike many other large landowners in our hometown, he did not do a lot of advance work to check where the deer were bedding down in the weeks leading up to the season. He had a couple of close friends for whom opening day was the most important day of the year. Another group of friends always camped for the two weeks of the season, so there was a fair amount of roughing it, playing cards, and then getting up early no matter what happened or how much alcohol had been consumed the night before.

Just about the time I started to walk, my dad gave me a turn-of-the-century single-shot lever-action 22 long rifle, which I still treasure today. He never properly instructed me in the art of the hunt or even told me hunting was basically a quiet activity.

So, as I grew up, he gave me bright clothing and told me to walk loudly at the highest point of the ridge, and to keep walking until I met up with our party on the other side of the mountain. Years later, I realized I had served as a human hunting dog, chasing deer off the ridge and into the path of hunters positioned across the mountain waiting for them. I distinctly remember four occasions when hunters shot deer during these times—deer that I never had a chance to see as I walked with my head down, making sure not to fall.

None of this, of course, changed that I was hunting. As we neared Thanksgiving, classmates in our rural one-room schoolhouse in central Vermont compared stories of their hunting experiences. Many of my classmates bagged their first deer before they were twelve years old.

No such luck for this ridge runner. I would not shoot a deer, or kill any animal larger than a woodchuck, until I was thirty-seven.

I may tell that story someday. For the time being, I will say that, in my opinion, a deer running through the woods has virtually no chance against a .30-30 rifle with a scope in the hands of anyone capable of firing the weapon. That was a big part of my decision, after this one particular experience, to eventually abandon rifle hunting as a sport altogether.

Always ready to learn something new, and not content hunting with my single-shot lever-action 22 long rifle, at fourteen I took up archery.

In my family, you needed to become completely proficient in any sport before you were provided with the right tools or equipment. So it was with some reluctance that my father bought me a used twenty-pound bow, three practice arrows, and two lethal-looking hunting arrows with a large quiver to hold them. I lobbied hard for more hunting arrows—wanting to give the appearance of Green Arrow—but Dad explained that if I was able to shoot even one arrow at a deer, I would have had the experience of a lifetime.

So, my father made a deal with me. I took the practice arrows out to the backyard and set up a target on a stack of hay with the goal to hit the target from a distance of forty feet. The reward was the right to include my two hunting arrows in the quiver and go on the hunt.

For most of the two weeks before the bow season opened, I went out there every day with my bow to shoot practice arrows at the target. Even on my worst day, I hit the bales of hay regularly and eventually the target. On the day my father certified me as an archer, he presented me with the quiver and my two razor-sharp hunting arrows.

I was confident that the first deer that came within range would be mine. I had only one last obstacle to overcome: getting out of bed on opening day.

I was clearly not a devoted hunter, and the first day of bow-and-arrow season, a Saturday, was cold and wet. I slept through the better part of the morning. My father commented only that I had probably missed the best opportunity to surprise the deer by getting up before dark and positioning myself in a place where I could shoot one. It rained harder on Sunday, so no one went out hunting.

At school Monday, many of my friends talked about their experiences hunting with their fathers. No one had actually shot at a deer, but everyone was excited about going out in the rain with the hope of seeing one.

Days grew shorter in the fall, and when school closed, I boarded the bus for home. I typically sat in the front and talked with the bus driver, Chunk, about my bow-hunting preparations.

As the bus rounded the corner toward our farm, Chunk pointed out two deer in the field on our property along the Dog River. Chunk said I should get my bow and arrows and go after the deer in the field as soon as I got home. He even dropped me off in front of our house instead of the bus stop at the Harlow Bridge School nearby to give me more time.

I ran to the porch, donned my boots and red tweed hunting jacket, and grabbed the new quiver with my two hunting arrows and my bow. I ran the fifty yards to the corner of the main road and nestled myself behind a tree to view the deer still casually eating in the field, oblivious to my presence.

I was out of breath, my heart pounded furiously, and I felt a cold sweat from the weight of the jacket and the full-out run from the house.

It was then that I realized that no one had taught me how to approach a deer with a bow and arrow. I'd never thought about crossing the thirty yards or so in an open field to get within range to shoot.

And it was beginning to get dark.

So, I began crawling across the field toward the grazing deer. I moved slowly and deliberately, on my stomach, and kept a low profile. As I think back about it now, it's amazing that I got within fifty feet of the deer without spooking them, but I was surely closer. It took me at least twenty minutes—blood pressure rising with anticipation, trying to hold my breath, making as little sound as possible.

When I felt I was close enough to chance a shot, I rose slowly to my knees, pulled one of the hunting arrows out of my quiver, drew the bow with all my might, and aimed for the shoulder of the smaller of the two deer closest to me.

I might have closed my eyes before I let the arrow fly. I remember the sloping arc that the arrow took as it rose up over the field and came to rest in the ground next to the front hoof of the deer.

There is a moment when you find yourself face-to-face with a live animal in the wild. If you are the hunter, anxiety rises within you— exhilaration, adrenaline—and for an instant, you feel more than human.

Like you have a superpower.

I can only imagine that for the hunted, the experience feels virtually the same. There's a moment of realization that you are face-to-face with a human, a sense of panic and danger rises up, and then you are faced with a logical decision to run away from the thing you fear most.

So it was with the deer that day. The larger deer hesitated, not quite realizing that someone had invaded her space. And while I do not recall if both deer immediately bolted away from me that day, it did not matter. I would not have a second shot, just as my father had told me.

Looking back over my shoulder after my lost opportunity, I saw a line of cars gathered along the side of the road, including Chunk in the bus and my father in his milk truck, all watching the entire episode unfold. At that point, whether the deer actually ran away mattered little. My seared memory recalls that the cars slowly started up, turned on their lights, and moved away as if the fireworks ended early and it was time to go home.

Hunting live animals may be a rite of passage and even necessary for survival depending on where you live. A vast amount of skill, along with a little luck, is necessary. Most of all, hunting requires a level of commitment. Like anything, without commitment, you might as well stick to ridge-running.

At dinner that evening, I discussed the hunting incident with my father. He didn't say much, as I recall, and I could not elaborate on the story because he'd watched it all from the comfort of his truck. He was concerned about the hunting arrow that was still stuck in the field and told me to get it back and to be sure that it was ready the next time I came across a deer in a field.

In the small town of Northfield, Vermont, the news of my great hunting excursion spread far and wide in the community of bus drivers and eventually to my hunting classmates. It was a little like *The Saturday Evening Post* cover where, at the beginning of the story,

I stalked two deer in the field, and at the end, I missed hitting any of the herd of thirty.

That might have been my last experience as a boy hunting with a bow and arrow, but much later in life, I took up the sport again. This time I had a powerfully sophisticated fifty-pound recurve hunting bow, a full quiver of arrows, and a camouflage suit. Deer had been seen bedding in the lower section of a large field on Winch Hill, which was owned by the former president of Norwich University, retired US Army major general W. Russell Todd, who encouraged me to come by some evening to set up in an old makeshift tree stand at the far end of the field.

To reach the tree, however, I would have to crawl across a large section of open and exposed field, much like I had so many years before. I did not make a sound as I approached the tree, swinging the bow across my shoulder and beginning the ten-foot climb up to the stand.

Over the course of the half hour or so that it took me to reach the tree, it started getting dark. As I took the last step up, the branch gave way and I hurtled straight down to the ground, trying to both tuck myself into a ball and reach for the bow and quiver to toss them to safety. I landed with a loud, crashing thud that must have echoed through the woods like a rifle shot.

It was a more than humbling waste of time. I am sure General Todd watched from his deck. And although nothing was seriously bruised or broken, I decided at that moment that my days as a hunter were over.

I find now that walks in an open field are the best thing I can do for myself. I am often on my way to or from a stream teeming with trout or walking along a path that leads to the stunning view of an autumn sunset.

It's times like these that I think about all the hours I have spent alone in a vast field, wondering about all of the stories that I want to share with you, old friend.

JUNE 15, 2012

CHAPTER 4

GETTING BY WITH SOME HELP FROM MY FRIENDS

I STARTED TO ASSEMBLE essays I had written after I attended a concert with Liz and Ann Hampton Callaway in Chicago. This memoir includes several letters I have written to their father, my late friend and mentor John Callaway, who passed away in June 2009 at age seventy-two after a fifty-two-year career in broadcast journalism in Chicago. He also served as an internet justice of the peace and married Denise and me on December 31, 2008.

The letters all start out the same way: "Dear John, I've been thinking a lot about . . ." and then we're off into some story, the end of which I rarely know. Eventually, I discover a point, remember lessons I have learned, reminisce about people I have met or who have influenced my life along the way, or rediscover a particular event worthy of writing about.

Through this process, I then discovered that one method to deal with grief and loss is to write. Often, those writings can take the form of letters—unfinished conversations, ideas, or thoughts. Grief provides an opportunity to pretend that those conversations continue; however, too often they play out as a series of voices in our minds rather than taking a shape that allows us to process them.

I don't recall when I actively chose to write down these conversations, but I do immediately write in times of despair or sadness. I am always better for writing it down and revisiting it from time to time.

Just like hearing from an old friend.

CHAPTER 5

NOTHING BUT NET— LIFE IS MAINTENANCE

A Review

John Callaway could have been a professional basketball player. Or a politician. Or even a columnist. But he admits to the audience at his delightful new one-man show, *Life is . . . Maintenance*, that dropping out of college is, in itself, a guarantee that none of those things will ever happen. So, what is left? Well, "maintenance"—and a lot of it.

You might not think, as you settle into the comfortable surroundings of the O'Rourke Center for the Performing Arts at Truman College, where Callaway opened his show last night, that the prime-time TV-personality-turned-Chicago-legend could captivate you so completely. The set could be any correspondent's study: piles of books, magazines and newspapers; file drawers and boxes; bookcases loaded with the treasures of a lifetime; clutter everywhere; and a bottle of water, which proves to be the only sustainable partner for Callaway on stage as he guides you through the two-plus hours of his amazing life journey.

He walks on stage, from out of the shadows, dribbling a basketball, taking shots at a hoop until, with the deftness of Michael Jordan, he swishes a three-pointer. Callaway then begins to define his life in several complex stages: his major addiction, "journalism"; all the minor ones (which are too numerous—and hilarious—to mention here); his fears; his many recognizable friends; and his wonderfully warm and loving view of the city of Chicago.

In Callaway's Chicago, there's Kup, Kalb, Studs, the Cubs, and Mayor Daley, the elder. He revisits The Drake, Rush Street and a host of old haunts in between in such a way that you can feel the atmosphere, hear the crackle of the crowd, and taste every delectable morsel. This is vintage Callaway, looking back at his twenty-eight-year-old self and knowing that, inside, he's aged only a day.

But outside, time has been an agent of change, and this provides for the evening's most frank and enjoyable moments. As Callaway recounts his daily medication requirements, their side effects and the mental state that taking them produces, you laugh right along with him at the futility of it all.

Those moments set you up for others of sobering reality—questions that we have all considered at one time or another about depression, success, failure or embarrassment. Callaway admits his bout with depression drove him to the edge but acknowledges that it was the encouragement of important people in his life that brought him back to form. That may be the most important message of many he wants you to take away from this piece; that is, to find some satisfaction in your life, you need to give a little of yourself to everyone you meet.

These are rich and fascinating stories, expertly delivered. You should run to see this wonderfully understated, honest and sincere performance by a man who is himself all those things, all at the same time.

MARCH 24, 2004

Act I, Scene 2

The game is changing
and your life is looking dreary.
Thank the Gorilla in the Room
You want to make believe you're
anything but weary.
Blame the Gorilla in the Room

Joe Gorilla
Act 1, Scene 2

Any way you look at it,
Chemotherapy sucks!
Not a thing compares to it,
Chemotherapy sucks!

Colin, Sam, and Edison
Act 1, Scene 2

CHAPTER 6

ACT I, SCENE 2

SETTING: Treatment Center Waiting Room

SONGS: GORILLA IN THE ROOM
              CHEMOTHERAPY SUCKS

AT RISE: In quick succession, under music, the
              ENSEMBLE walks on the revolving-stage
              track to a hospital waiting room with
              chairs and other patients present.
              Each of the principals gets in line
              for check-in; one by one they pick up
              documents and move off to complete them
              as the crossover music transitions.

The stage track revolves back to the elevator. All
action onstage freezes; the doors open; and JOE
GORILLA and the CHAOSALS enter. JOE sings GORILLA
IN THE ROOM.

The CHAOSALS raise havoc (misplacing items,
unhanging coats, etc.) in the waiting room during
the number.

As JOE concludes, DR. THOMPSON enters the tableau. He is consumed by his work and oblivious to the actions of JOE and the CHAOSALS.

As JOE exits with the CHAOSALS, the stage action immediately resumes. The COMPANY on stage sees the havoc. DR. THOMPSON, startled at recognizing JOE and the CHAOSALS, exits.

The waiting room returns to normal as the IMPATIENT PATIENT enters in a wheelchair with assistance from an ORDERLY. They make their way to the admissions area and take their place behind SAM, who asks the attendant about his treatment.

In the middle of the discussion, the IMPATIENT PATIENT whacks SAM with his cane.

SAM asks what is wrong, and the ORDERLY tells him he is taking too long. SAM apologizes and turns back to the attendant.

The IMPATIENT PATIENT whacks him with his cane.

SAM is perturbed but composes himself and attempts to finish the conversation. As the IMPATIENT PATIENT tries to whack him a third time, SAM steps out of the way and traps the cane against the admission table. He finishes his discussion as the IMPATIENT PATIENT tries in vain to free the cane from SAM's grasp.

JACK returns to KATHARINE with his documents.

A conversation between patients COLIN, SAM, and EDISON leads into the song CHEMOTHERAPY SUCKS, during which three nurses escort patients into another area where the nurses take blood samples, weigh them, and prep them for treatment.

The stage track rotates to reveal a chemotherapy treatment ward with large, comfortable chairs, as well as IV stands with bags and hoses. The nurses scurry about, aligning the treatment apparatus and tending to the patients.

The number ends as the treatments begin.

                    BLACKOUT

CHAPTER 7

THE CLUB

BY NOW, YOU PROBABLY know that I have recently joined a special "Club" of people who are battling cancer. You play the cards you are dealt, remain positive, and make the most of every day you have. Each one of us in the "Club" knows that—now more than ever.

Club admittance came as quite a surprise following a routine colonoscopy on June 30, 2008. At my fiftieth birthday party in 2004, my surgeon friend gave me a "Time to get checked!" card. That card still has a special place at home. And while it took almost four years for me to take action—and some of this might have been avoided by earlier detection—my case is like every case of cancer: unique to the individual.

That last part is critically important. I have waited until now—about a third of the way through my chemotherapy treatment—to reflect on what happened thus far and how I am coping with this disease.

I thought I would read everything about cancer online. I gave up in less than an hour on day one after I quickly realized none of it applied to me. My medical team confirmed this fact.

"Listen to me," said my surgeon, a personal friend and nationally recognized gastroenterologist. "Rule No. 1: Nobody's cancer journey is the same."

And so I listened to him. For the next seventeen days until my surgery, I single-mindedly focused on an array of work, family, and life issues to get ready for an unexpected four-week hiatus as I recovered at home. My life, for the first time in a decade, was almost completely in order—and I felt a great deal of satisfaction and accomplishment.

And fear of the unknown.

While I had taken care of virtually every aspect of my life that might cause unnecessary stress, I couldn't prepare for what I didn't know.

To this point, I could only imagine how most people react when a doctor tells them the result of any routine test is not good and that surgery will be necessary. Having a long-planned fishing adventure within a six-week window of my surgery, my first question was if I could go. Assured that I could make the trip if I followed all instructions, I asked the next big question: What about aftercare?

"You likely won't need any," I learned. "Oh, and you'll probably lose thirty to forty pounds, perhaps more."

That didn't sound so bad.

"You'll have a big scar," my surgeon said, "but you should look okay in a swimsuit."

Perfect, I thought. Don't go to the beach and no longer swim.

So, a couple of weeks after the diagnosis, I was admitted to Northwestern Hospital with Denise by my side, under the care of a team of experts. The nurses prepped me for what I termed my "punctuation surgery," which would take me from a "colon" to a "semi-colon." That was the last thing I said to the surgical staff before they put me under. One of my spiritual friends said that I should think positive thoughts throughout this process, so I had saved that one for the operating room.

Modern surgery is a moment in time.

I remember my surgeon saying, "Everything is fine," as his team wheeled me away. I drifted in and out of consciousness over the next several hours. I knew when Denise was in the room. I did not know much else, except where the pain-relief button was on the bed. I pushed it often those first few hours.

I remember little.

Over the next five days, I had excellent care. The goal was to get up and walk almost immediately. An overachiever, if they wanted two laps around the floor, I did four. If they wanted six, I did nine.

On day three, the pathology report came back. I had a sense that morning that the news would be bad. The hint was confirmed when I was supposed to hear by 11 a.m., and the news did not come until just after 1 p.m.

I would need more consultations.

I would need more answers.

OCTOBER 5, 2008

CHAPTER 8

GORILLA IN THE ROOM

I FIRST IMAGINED *Gorilla in the Room*, a masterpiece destined to be my second Broadway musical—I gave up on the first one—as what if *Crazy for You* met *How to Succeed in Business Without Really Trying* and *On the Waterfront*. Lots of songs, high comedy, and laugh-a-minute situations in a rough-and-tough fight for your life.

The show logo—a gorilla's hand holding up a title card—and a stunning logline came first: "Members of a special club join together to overcome a formidable foe."

Soon after, the arc of the story gushed out in one night. It was a mangled train wreck of a musical comedy written by a cancer patient during chemotherapy treatments for the pure enjoyment of other cancer patients and caregivers who knew the inside story.

Set in an urban treatment center in the present day, act I unfolds over the course of one late-fall day. The center serves cancer fighters, and in the opening number we meet the protagonist, Dr. Thompson, an oncologist, and four patients—and caregivers—arriving for treatment. We also meet the mysterious, all-knowing presence, Joe Gorilla, a larger-than-life song-and-dance man, and his minions, the Chaosals (pronounced KAY-AH-SOLS), who enter and leave throughout the course of the action, raising havoc at every opportunity. As the characters' personal cancer journeys unfold, the center itself becomes a patient, fighting for survival as a bottom-line administrator and the center's board grapple with the inevitable closure of the facility and the prospect of moving patient care to a massive regional center fifty miles away. The intersection of Dr. Thompson's passion to keep the center open and provide services to his patients with Joe Gorilla's challenging message of courage and hope are at the core of the story. I imagined the rehearsals unfolding dozens of times as I sat in various seat locations in the theater. I looked forward to the next night's imaginary rehearsal as a safe place to go, sometimes for hours, to rework choreography, rewrite a song, or sketch a piece of scenery that needed to move on and offstage.

I'd wake up often from a nap with a pencil still in my hand, and then I'd immediately dive back in.

The team of specialists who treated me in July 2008 may have been a bit skeptical at first. But as six months of bi-monthly chemotherapy treatments progressed into January 2009, the musical served as a hopeful, even invigorating, exercise when I felt otherwise exhausted.

My own personal "waiting room" expanded over the summer, fall, and early spring. Instead of having conversations in person, I escaped into the past and wrote about other people who had and were making a difference in my life. Outside of work conversations, I became a student of listening to others and reveling in the sound of their voices and what they were saying to me. Looking back now, it seems that I often treated each conversation as if it were the last one.

That touch of finality is hard to understand unless you are in "the Club"—by my definition, those who have or have had any form of cancer in their lifetime and who live by a few simple "rules." I discovered that once the important things I needed to do each day were complete—taking care of loved ones, work, medical treatments—I was left with only free time to muse about the future or the need to completely shut down.

So, it became important for me to use the free time wisely, and that compelled me to write every idea down. After a while, the treatments interrupted my ability to write or type, so I took an alternate route that is a big part of this story all those years ago.

To this day I am not sure if any of the dozens of professionals involved in my care actually thought that a musical about my cancer journey might someday make it to the stage, but they were so highly skilled and experienced that they allowed me—as I am sure they allow every other member of "the Club"—whatever latitude was necessary to get to the other side of treatment.

And no one has ever noticed that my gorilla-hand logo has no thumb.

MARCH 31, 2020

CHAPTER 9

PEOPLE I KNEW— JAMES VELVET WIMSATT

Better music ne'er was known,
Than a choir of hearts in one.
Let each other, that hath been
Troubled with the gall or spleen,
Learn of us to keep his brow
Smooth and plain, as ours are now.
Sing, though, before the hour of dying,
He shall rise, and then be crying,
"Hey, ho, 'tis nought but mirth
That keeps the body from the earth!"

The Knight of the Burning Pestle
Francis Beaumont and John Fletcher
1607

JAMES VELVET, AN ACCOMPLISHED musician, songwriter, radio personality, activist, and poet, was known to me as James Wimsatt during our college years. James was a tall, affable, lumbering young thespian when we met in 1973. He walked tilted somewhat awkwardly forward, his feet flapping down a bit with each step, arms straight and hands generally still by his side, except to brush the long, brown hair out of his eyes. He wore tattered T-shirts under denim work shirts, faded jeans, and work boots rarely laced, as did we all. He was the original aristocat—no r.

I am sure he smoked, although I cannot recall it being an abusive habit. I sensed that he was a frugal spender, but never cheap and always generous with whatever he had, particularly jaunts in the offbeat VW Thing he drove around campus. I am equally sure he drank, probably to excess like the rest of us, since there were nights when we spent hours with a large group of theater folk, holding court with James, Terry Demas, and others at a famous Burlington haunt called the Chez Dufais. Court was in session roughly twenty minutes after rehearsal's end till closing.

I remember the entrances much more clearly than the exits in those days. Early arrivals gathered tables and chairs together, and soon the room was abuzz with more than a dozen loud, boisterous voices. As in all elements of theater, there was context, pace, suspense, humor, and "a button" on every story as we floated into an alcohol-induced comic, classic, and political seminar.

James was clearly several years older but still an undergraduate at the University of Vermont. I recall James as an expert in music, physical comedy, commedia dell'arte, the classics, Shakespeare, film, and comedians, as well as being an astute writer and editor—a skill that must have been acquired long before his UVM days. He professed that comedy is based on the "rule of three," and that "repetition is the essence of comedy."

"There are three players in Elizabethan comedy," James would say, "three clowns in a circus, and three sisters in Chekov!"

"Ahhh, not a comedy, James."

"Just checking to see if you're paying attention." He continued, "Three in a nuclear family, a successful ménage à trois, and three on a match!"

"Again, not such a rewarding experience for the third guy on the match."

"Well, it's not 'two on a match,' not 'five sheets to the wind.' It's all about the number three, right down to how many glasses of wine are enough and how many white pizzas ensure that there will be something left to take home."

White pizza!?!

We were first cast together in Ionesco's *Macbett*, directed by Charles Towers. We played Glamiss and Candor, two Scotsmen who open the show by hatching a plot to overthrow the king. Our patter was meant to set the pace for the entire show. We entered in our best business kilts (with briefcases), took our places in imaginary twentieth-century office spaces on a barren, multi-level stage, discussing the foreshadowing of the story by telephone—not once looking at each other until we took an oath of allegiance at the tip of each other's dueling swords. During the photo shoot, we playfully stabbed each other in the groin. Regrettably, James had longer arms than I did.

While the character James played died heroically in battle offstage, I was captured and brought before the tribunal to recite a marvelous death speech early in the play. James helped direct that speech by telling me, "It is the funniest two minutes in the play. Just stand there and say the lines."

He was right. On opening night my death scene was hilarious. I then spent the next few nights trying to improve it, with disastrous results. So, I went back to James and asked him what had happened.

"Ed. It's the funniest two minutes in the play. Just stand there and say the lines. Oh, and make sure people can hear you."

White pizza!?!

Weeks later, James was tapped to direct a mainstage production of Beaumont and Fletcher's *The Knight of the Burning Pestle*—a high honor. He cast me as Old Master Merrythought, and I joined a cast who had considerably more classical training and an abundance of natural comedic timing. The adaptation that James developed is a play within a play, a Don Quixote tale of love and entanglements.

According to James, who wanted to keep things simple, Merrythought enters at various times and speaks directly to the audience, chiding them to "loosen up, be merry, enjoy the show, get with it." When I asked about my character's motivation, he shook his head, gave me a big sigh, and lumbered off.

Apparently, I took comedy seriously in those days.

The theater created a blank canvas for James and all the rest of his art supplies. I find it hard to imagine any undergraduate student in theater today choosing to mount such an ambitious production on their own. The script was dense, the characters extreme, and the actors, lights, costumes, and set made such a brilliant visual tapestry that the play would appear to the audience as spring itself when it opened in mid-April.

Everything about *Pestle* was capital BIG—the stage was raked and elevated from four to over eight feet high, filling the downstage thrust area of the theater and incorporating colorful revolving back panels upstage. Each act had wild consequences, music, and props true to the era. Altogether, it was surely a Staye Loose Production— the generational faux production company handed down over the course of several years as homage to past University Players.

James allowed great freedom to actors to stretch into a role. He ran double-time rehearsals to get the dialogue jump-started. These speed drills helped calibrate the production and identify trouble areas of blocking and movement, on and offstage. We would reevaluate a particular sequence if the players couldn't make a costume change during a speed drill. It was all about rhythm and pace.

For Merrythought, I wore a fat suit and had a large bunch of plastic grapes strapped to my belt buckle that swayed from one side to the other on every step. I carried real grapes in a pouch alongside and real wine in a wine sleeve over my shoulder. Even then, since Merrythought had no clever repartee or comedic shtick, there was no apparent humor in the part. As opening night loomed, I felt flat and otherwise ineffective. At one point, I thought that James might recast me. I was so insecure that I approached him about moving me out of the role.

James immediately focused the conversation away from recasting but told me it was apparent that I was not having fun. He said what I was doing felt like work to him when so many of my other roles had a free spirit. It looked like I was afraid of making a mistake. Artists who live that way, he said, make more mistakes than anyone.

The answer for that first weekend was to be as big as possible. Challenge the audience. Get in their face. Be loud and boisterous. Single people out and come back to them throughout the night. Force them to smile and laugh. Raise their spirits and then let the rest of the cast coddle them with mirth and merriment for the rest of the show. *Pestle* was written to break the fourth wall, and Merrythought led the way. James reasoned that, with three shows the first weekend, an outdoor performance, and three more the following weekend, we had time to adjust to the audience as things developed.

On opening night, in a warm, friendly, packed house, *Pestle* was dubbed an unqualified success. The whimsical set designed by Lisa Devlin, along with colorful lights and costumes, framed the extraordinary performances of Charles Towers, Sarah Brooke, Peter Kurth, and Jonathan Bourne. The rest of the superb ensemble played well, and Merrythought passably enticed the audience into laughter at every opportunity, without a single laugh line of his own.

Overall, the success of *Pestle*'s opening weekend was satisfying. There were, however, four shows left to go, and the next one was outdoors in April, when spring can be quite fickle in Vermont. James prepped us well and gave superb notes on our performance. He was careful to praise actors' successes and, in most cases, ignore areas that he could not resolve. When we talked privately, he was more adamant than ever that I was on the right path but not there yet. It still seemed that I was working too hard and that this should be an easy role for me, but he could not tell me specifically what was missing. He wanted fun, gaiety, and laughter from everyone involved. I must have appeared like Hamlet in need of grape reduction.

Little did I know what was in store the following Thursday. I recall it as the happiest day of my young life to that date. Our troupe poured out onto what is now officially named the Piazza Della Feidner on a beautifully dry and warm spring day. There were hundreds on hand to watch, and it was perfect weather for wine. Merrythought no longer was confined to the dark inner walls of the theater. There was an immediate rousing connection with the audience, and Merrythought now joined them in the joy of the show, sat down in the audience between appearances, shared real wine from the sleeve with patrons, and cajoled the audience into uproarious laughter. A chord was struck that day, and from the moment that we stepped onto the piazza to the moment we took our bows, the exhilarating feeling never went away. James was thrilled that nature had taken its course and, I am sure, helped define this wonderful character within me.

Directing, I learned from my friend James, is being a good editor, storyteller, traffic cop, father, mother, girlfriend or boyfriend, taskmaster, and teacher. No matter what happens, there is always a following action. All you need to do is get to the next one in the most entertaining way possible until the play is done.

James told a joke about the King's Cup. Not surprisingly, you have to begin the joke three times throughout a long drinking session, raising suspense and curiosity, and heightening the hilarious ending. If you have never heard the touching King's Cup story, all you need to remember is that epic comedy requires patience and that you should "always drink from this side of the cup!"

Cheers to you, my friend.

MAY 1, 2015

• JAMES VELVET WIMSATT •
March 29, 1950—April 17, 2015

CHAPTER 10

THANK YOU AND GOOD NIGHT

JOHN CALLAWAY WALKED INTO the construction scene at the Pritzker Military Library in July 2003 with his friend Libbet Richter. Libbet showed off what she was sure would be the next impressive new cultural institution in Chicago to Mr. Callaway. She also wanted to introduce me, a newcomer to Chicago and the new founding director of the library. I had been in town less than a year.

John stepped nimbly around the construction debris and the massive prairie-style sconces that were being lifted to the ceiling, and he raised his eyebrows when he saw the seven-by-fifteen-foot video production room where we planned, later that fall, to broadcast live, with audience, full-format video of book talks, panels, and lectures on the internet.

John leaned in at this point, laser-focused on a potential series of panel discussions that might include edgy, current themes about industrial and medical innovations by the military in time of war; social and geopolitical commentary from Chicago-based opinion makers; and historical examinations of conflicts from the veterans who fought them.

It was clear to me that he and Libbet had already been talking.

Then John sent in a zinger that caught me flat-footed.

"So, what's on your agenda?" he asked.

"I don't have an agenda," I said, thinking he meant politics. "I'm just hoping to tell compelling stories."

"Well," he said, "I have always thought that the best stories start with a solid plan, a unique point of view, and lots of options in mind so you won't be too surprised when things don't work out the way you thought they would."

Later that night, doing my research after the introduction rather than before, I realized with great embarrassment that I had spent the previous two hours with a legend of broadcasting and journalism.

That meeting changed my life forever and we became fast friends.

Every hour spent with John Callaway—in person, on the phone, or watching him work—I learned something essential. He was the consummate interviewer and a fascinating storyteller: direct and energetic, with a vast depth of knowledge. Often he'd call himself a "generalist," but there was so much more in John Callaway than anyone will ever know. He only showed this wonderful humble side on those occasions. He was one of the smartest and most caring people I knew . . . and the best conversationalist.

He loved reading, learning, and listening—three traits that are all but nonexistent in our multi-second media society. He did not accept first assumptions, listened to the reply of a guest instead of sticking to whatever plan he had carefully forged, and consistently produced award-winning journalistic reports, interviews, and stories about Chicago's rich and colorful history and its impact across the nation and the world.

John looked up from the chaos of the Pritzker Military Library on that July 2003 day and said, "If you can finish this thing and get it online by October 23, good sir, I'll recommend that you be sent to Iraq to clean up that mess!"

We did, but the call overseas never came.

The service call never came for John Callaway as a young man, either. But he came on board enthusiastically for our opening, and then he joined us on what would be a run of more than five years on *Front & Center with John Callaway* at the library—his fifty-fifth program just last month. In our interview together when the library honored him with their Founders Award two years ago, he recalled his boyhood memory of the bombing of Pearl Harbor that thrust us into World War II, the fear he felt for the future, and the understanding that the train set he would receive for Christmas that year might be the last toy he received for many years to come. And it was.

He spent his early professional years in a family of writers and publishers; sold newspapers on the street as a boy, developing as a journalist; arrived in Chicago "with seventy-one cents in his pocket," a story he freely admits was more prose than proof; and, through some classic twists of fate and good old hard work, landed a job at the City News Bureau of Chicago, which helped shape his writing and reporting skills, and forged some serious lifelong relationships with the greats of Chicago media. Those early years were difficult but stimulating, and when he spoke of them, there was a glow in his eye for a time and a Chicago gone by. Callaway earned a reputation as an inquisitive beat reporter, covering the intense stories of the turbulent 1960s with skill and compassion, always living the line, "If your mother says she loves you, check it out!"

He would be known for many things, but radio loved his voice, and so did we. John Callaway took his skills to the ever-expanding network market, in New York with CBS, and then back to Chicago where he became the television host of *Chicago Tonight* and covered all the news and interviewed everyone who was anyone who came to the city.

When I met John, he had left *Chicago Tonight* and was arguably in the twilight of his extraordinary broadcast career. While he was producing the second of his two brilliant one-man shows and making the *Chicago Stories* features on WTTW, he wanted to do more. We asked and he gladly committed to host a monthly public affairs panel on military topics at the library, with Libbet serving as producer. From the very beginning in January 2003, John's professionalism raised the bar of our programs. At the time, the shows looked a little like an early version of television, but quickly, our production team, led by Dan Thompson, Andrew Edeker and David Canneck, solved major production problems, and we secured a broadcast spot on WYCC, a public broadcast station in Chicago, which became the television broadcast home for all of our programs.

Front & Center was nominated for a Chicago Midwest-Emmy Award in 2008—the first time a library has ever received such an honor. It was a proud moment for all of us at the library. But it was all about the man, our friend John Callaway, who always led the way, challenged our thinking, and tried to move the program up the cultural ladder with more insightful debates and controversial topics.

In recent years, he had been busier than ever, leading a wonderful weekly interview program called *Friday Night with John Callaway* on WTTW. In the middle of his fifty-second year in this business, he left the way he would want to: planning for another interview and developing a panel on the challenges facing combat journalists in this economy.

"I was born to interview," John once told me.

I will never forget that.

John Callaway will leave a tremendous void in the creation of intelligent, learned debate in our business. He was funny, direct, extremely well read, and one of the most decent men I have ever known. I love him and I'll miss him very much.

John, thank you and good night.

JUNE 24, 2009

• JOHN CALLAWAY •
August 22, 1936—June 23, 2009

Act I, Scene 3

Hope is always warm and special
Hope is trying to understand
I want only to be with you
And keep us all together, so
Hope grows, even for a moment
Hope lasts, longer than a day,
I pray we will find a way to carry on
And make our moments last.

Mother Terone
Act I, Scene 3

ACT I, SCENE 3

SETTING: Treatment Waiting Room

SONG: HOPE

AT RISE: In the waiting room, MOTHER TERONE
             joins TESS and TOSS.

TESS is the patient. MOTHER tries to take charge
of the situation, speaking to the admissions
attendant.

As the conversation escalates, the IMPATIENT PATIENT
approaches the admissions desk. KATHARINE steps
in just as the ORDERLY wheels off the IMPATIENT
PATIENT and into the treatment area.

KATHARINE, JACK, CLINT, and JILL sing HOPE, joined
by TESS, TOSS, and MOTHER.

As the song concludes, the treatment doors open and
a nurse signals that it is time for them to enter.

BLACKOUT

CHAPTER 12

BE POSITIVE

I WAS DIAGNOSED WITH stage 3C colon cancer.

Five of the sixteen lymph nodes were malignant. My surgeon removed those nodes, along with 20 percent of my colon. The good news? It was completely contained and gone. I would, however, need chemotherapy to provide better odds against anything reoccurring in the future. The long-term prognosis was simple and vague: three years, thumbs-up; five years, pop the champagne!

Following major surgery, but feeling only marginally better than I did a few days before, the news was numbing. While I had mentally prepared for the surgery and had been hopeful about the overall result and incredibly diligent in getting back on my feet, I could feel the air being sucked from my lungs.

Worse, the news was devastating to Denise, who never showed me one moment of emotion. I am sure she spent hours on her own wrestling with all of the various outcomes.

Later that day, the friendly neighborhood oncologist came for a visit. He wasted no time.

"This is not a death sentence," he said. "You can do this thing. This is not your father's chemotherapy."

He then looked me square in the eye.

"Ed, you are going to die of something, someday, but it won't be this," he said. "We will beat this thing."

"Will I be able to go on my fishing trip?" I asked.

After a brief discussion about dates, he said, "Let's go for it."

Someone told me that Ronald Reagan said, after his colon cancer surgery, "I had cancer there once. They took it out and now it's gone."

I have never forgotten that, and it is Rule No. 2: Remain incredibly positive.

CHAPTER 13

COMFORT FOOD— A RECIPE FOR MOTHER'S DAY

ONLY SOMEONE AS RESOURCEFUL as my mother could unite an old Pyrex casserole dish with a brown-cow cookie jar and make them work together. Both had a special place in my mother's kitchen and were the source of an almost endless stream of delectable edibles in my youth. As I reflected on this Mother's Day, and thought about the comfort and support all mothers provide for their families, I dug out that old casserole dish, placed it on the kitchen counter, and admired it.

While it is easy to list all the guiding values our mothers gave to us—how to act in public and how to tell right from wrong, as well as clarifying and elaborating on what your father might have forgotten to tell you about how to treat a lady—try as I may, it will take me more than the twenty years since her passing to sort out all the good advice given simply from her nurturing spirit and love of life. The vivid memories of kindness to everyone she knew—and didn't know; her emotional strength of will in trying times; and her patience and understanding of teenage rebellion all stand out. Her love of nature, art, and music are the gifts I cherish most.

And then there was the love for home cooking. I mean, really good comfort food!

What's in the kitchen?

"Plenty of everything," she would say.

Donuts, hot from the old tin pan and bubbling with scalding Crisco oil, almost every other Sunday. Sheets of rolled donut batter popping out a pile of perfect holes, many of which would never make it to the cooker. Every kind of homemade pie bursting with all the fresh fruits you can imagine—and some I didn't even know existed— ready to eat almost every day, sometimes appearing overnight. And everything you can make from chocolate: chocolate chip cookies, chocolate cake with chocolate frosting, chocolate brownies, without nuts, and even fresh chocolate milk. I remember hovering over the frosting pan before it made its way to the sink, hopeful that, in addition to the two small spoonsful of pure chocolate purposely left for me, it would somehow produce a fresh pan of fudge as I made my way home from school the next day.

It mystifies me that she did this while raising four kids eleven years apart, working full time, volunteering for various community and women's organizations, serving as transportation coordinator for many of our extracurricular activities, and acting as seamstress, accountant, and room inspector for our family. I do not recall my mother ever missing a recital, concert, or any other important public event we participated in. I am sure she did; I just can't recall any now. She wanted to support just about everyone and everything that happened in our small Vermont town. She was the original Energizer Bunny.

It is now clear to me that my mom and dad nurtured us through food. No matter what season it was in Vermont, the next meal of the day—and the one after that—was important. Growing up on a farm, we had fresh beef, chicken, eggs, milk, corn on the cob, carrots, peas, and beets fresh from a bountiful summer garden. Mom and Dad toiled over a large patch of raspberry bushes and an enormous asparagus bed, and they competed in the neighborhood challenge for the first radish of the season.

My parents would spend midsummer nights together weeding and then preserving the crop for the winter, so that sometime in late January, we'd dine on potatoes, corn, and a big roast pork from our freezer, to the delight of my father, who would remind us how lucky we were despite the twenty-below weather. He always thanked Mom for the good meal. They'd often wash dishes together.

No holiday went by without food for everyone to take home. My mother wanted to be sure that if you entered our house hungry, you left waddling through the door.

On the day before Mother's Day 2010, I awoke thinking about all the comfort food my mother must have served out of that Pyrex casserole dish. Even more was stored in her brown-cow cookie jar on the kitchen counter. Long ago, my sister, Tracy, a nickname from her youth, and I agreed to disagree on the two most important items in mother's kitchen. That is when I received the casserole dish; she got the brown cow.

My thoughts drifted back to all the school lunches, bake sales, neighborhood gatherings, meals for the families of friends in need, and the vibrant memory of four unruly kids huddled around the small table in the kitchen with salmon pea wiggle (peas and canned salmon mixed in a milk gravy—a throwback to the days before iceboxes, and familiar to New Englanders) or a hearty beef stew. Things seemed to naturally come together in my mother's kitchen. It was a place where every smell could keep you eagerly waiting for her call: "Wash your hands! Dinner's ready!"

Of all the comfort food I longed for most, I had been unable to conjure up, on my own, my mother's macaroni and cheese casserole recipe. Macaroni and cheese is a rather simple dish. However, whenever I made it, it was substantially different from my mom's. Something was missing, and today was to be the day to figure it out.

In the spirit of full disclosure, I need to state that, although I consider myself a competent cook, my sister has forgotten more about cooking, baking, and feeding people than I will ever hope to know. She was the one who paid attention all those years ago to our mother and grandmother, and she, too, is an accomplished professional businesswoman and mother of three. Unlike my sister, I have never successfully recreated my mother's expert touch in pies, cakes, cookies, or the famous macaroni and cheese, despite having all of the right ingredients at my disposal and the alpha Pyrex vessel she made it in.

I was too busy eating to watch.

I guess I always felt that there is magic in what mothers do for their children. Rarely do they even know what that magic is . . . or that it is happening.

Each year, in the weeks leading up to Mother's Day, I realize I could not possibly send cards or notes to all of those women who have a special place in my life. I could not call them all personally or write everything I want to say on this important day. I try to do that throughout the year. I miss the mark and get wrapped up in my own life sometimes, but like any good mother would do, these women remind me often that they are there with their own cards and notes, thinking good thoughts and sending a prayer for me and my family. They have made me feel like a favorite son all of my adult life.

They each know who they are and how much I love them because I tell them so.

And on my special mothers list this year are my daughter, Amanda, who is the mother of my granddaughter, Allie Kate—the most wonderful miracle in our lives; my sweet and loving mother-in-law, Diane, who reminds me every day that I am her favorite—and only—son-in-law; and my sister, who made this Mother's Day extra special for me.

You see, I went online and found a 1958 Pyrex Golden Hearts 2.5-Quart Cinderella casserole dish identical to my mother's coveted workhorse. The description said, "Just like new!" and it was surprisingly affordable. I made sure that it would be sent to my sister directly, perhaps in time for Mother's Day, but that didn't really matter, since she's out of town. Once the sale was complete, I called my sister to tell her about my find and the rest of the story of how frustrated I was in not getting the recipe right all these years later.

Being the wonderful person that she is, my sister shared with me the secret of my mother's recipe. With the "just like new" dish on its way to her home, I only wish I could see the look in her eyes when the dish and cow are reunited—a symbolic yet significant gesture on her younger brother's part to make a Mother's Day complete.

(I did not suggest to her that the brown-cow cookie jar is very available—and a highly collectible and expensive item online—or that, perhaps on a future Father's Day, a cow cookie jar might find its way to me somehow.)

The rest of the story is predictable: I set off to buy the ingredients, confident that I was on the verge of preparing the best macaroni and cheese in years. It was. And Mom would have been very proud. There's plenty left for today.

What we call "comfort food" is all about memory.

My mother left this very casserole dish brimming with macaroni and cheese in the freezer a couple of days before she passed. On another Mother's Day, twenty years ago today, our family enjoyed a meal together made by her hands one last time. The dish serves now as a warm and heartfelt memory of other times, when all we wanted to hear was "Wash your hands. Dinner's ready!"

Whether you are a mother, married to one, or have one you are celebrating with today, happy Mother's Day!

To all the mothers who pass along their pride and love to their children and never quite know if it makes a difference, I can tell you that, no matter what you may think, we're watching, listening, learning, and growing every time you say our names, look our way, or do the magical things that mothers do.

There is no greater gift than a mother's love and no greater memory than the look in her eyes when you say to her, "I love you, Mom."

Or, "I'll do the dishes!"

MAY 9, 2010

• HELEN E. TRACY •
December 6, 1923—December 15, 1989

Postscript: On or around Father's Day 2010, a package arrived with a pristine brown-cow cookie jar that has now been reunited with the alpha Pyrex casserole dish—a gift from my wife, Denise. My sister, whom I love dearly, told me later that she had taken one look at the online price for the item and decided, instead, to ship a month's supply of cookies and the recipes.

CHAPTER 14

MOTHER'S DAY—
TO MY DAUGHTER

Dear Amanda:

I've been meaning to write you this letter for a long time.

The last few months have been interesting. I had expected that completing the chemotherapy treatment would be satisfying. The two-week sessions were not fun to look forward to, and certainly not enjoyable to live through. I realize that if it were not for the love and support of many people near me—and those sending prayers and good thoughts from afar—I would not have fared nearly as well.

So, I decided, leading up to Mother's Day 2009, to sit back and write my daughter a letter to let her know how proud I am of what she has done to make my world—and my life—so much better.

When you consider everything that has happened to our family in the last two and a half to three years, it almost defies any novel or movie-script treatment. From my perspective, I transitioned out of a job I love as executive director of the library to focus my efforts on the foundation, only to, in the last several months, transition out of that job to take on new responsibilities in the organization. There is tremendous faith in my abilities, but I'm sure there are now—for the first time in my career—also questions about my future health and stability. I have them myself, so I should not think that any organization would not look at me and wonder if everything will be okay.

I learned a long time ago there are no guarantees in life. So I do not worry about what I have not accomplished in the past or what may ultimately happen in the future. I'd rather try to absorb and consume the present.

Throughout the last few years, I have seen some amazing things, but none compare with everything that you have done since mid-June two years ago to support your daughter, to forge ahead and make a new professional life for yourself.

Any father would be happy to have a daughter who has done only a small portion of what you've done in your short life. You are an exceptional writer; you're a strongly positive and energetic person. You're exceptionally good with people, and you can see through a project to find what's important and real about it. Above all, you have a passion for the work that you do.

I admire the passion that you have now for your work with the March of Dimes, for raising your beautiful daughter, and for the new life you are building. Who knows what the future will hold for any of us? I've had an exceptionally good life and expect to be around for many, many decades to come. I wanted to be sure that before whatever happens does, I have taken at least one brief moment and one quiet time in my life to reflect and write to you and tell you how absolutely proud I am of your work, your energy, and your love of life. Don't ever lose that. These are your most endearing qualities, and I love you all the more for them.

Not long ago, I came across a letter my mother wrote to me. It was nothing like the letter that she wrote to my brother Paul during her enlightenment period, which stands alone as a singularly superb piece of prose and was read at her funeral. Her letter to me was an honest glimpse of who she was—a moment when my mother took the time to tell me who she saw that day, who she'd spoken with on the phone, and what was important to her. She made a point of telling me that she was happy to see me, happy to hear our voices when we called, and most of all, appreciated some gifts I'd sent to her in recent weeks. But in the end, it was just a note from her—a moment in time that I have treasured all these years.

There were many of these notes. If I started in earnest tomorrow, she has already outdone me, or anything I could hope to accomplish in this area, in her short lifetime. Emails are not quite the same. They are abrupt, quick blasts of thought that, on the surface, may appear quite informative, but something is missing. Perhaps it is that the passion of the writing needs to be expressed either by hand or on an old IBM Selectric—with Wite-Out and any corrections on the only copy produced. An original, with little afterthought or attempts to squeeze in some excess emphasis . . . or another qualifier . . . (*like this last one!*)

I, of course, did not write this on an IBM Selectric. I have thought about buying an old typewriter because, not long ago, I received a typewritten letter and enjoyed it very much. Rather—and I think my mother would be impressed—I dictated this in a MacSpeech program as I lay comfortably back in bed, quite unable to type this evening because my hands don't feel like doing the motions that they have done for so many years. But there is a freedom in dictation. While I miss being creative instantaneously, I'm getting used to the fact that I can dictate my thoughts and have them come out reasonably well the first time through.

Best of all, perhaps, is that I let the person who I'm writing to know that it was important for me to stop, take the time, and tell them what I thought.

I'm thinking that I love you very much, and I wanted you to know. You can try to make me prouder of you than you already have, but I don't think that's possible. I've always been very proud and loved you very, very much. That will never change because you are a very special person.

Your grandmother ended each letter the same way. She'd write, "Love always."

She was a very special person, too.

MAY 9, 2009

CHAPTER 15

CALL YOUR MOTHER. SHE WORRIES.

MY MOTHER-IN-LAW, Diane Marie (Hertwig) McGowan, who passed on February 15, often mentioned in our conversations that I was her favorite son-in-law.

I'd remind her that I was her only son-in-law.

I alternated "Diane" and "Mom," which never seemed to bother her, although I confess now that I always felt intimidated using "Mom" around any of the other five "real" sons.

If I had it to do all over again, I'd ask permission to call her "Mom." I wonder now what she might have said. "Of course you can!" Or maybe in mixed family company she'd say, "Everyone calls me Diane."

Most everyone did.

Come to think of it, when I spoke with her, she rarely ever used my name.

Diane would talk about what was happening with the other family members—sisters, sons, grandchildren—her favorite television shows, scores of movies, or events that occurred years ago in the old neighborhood, in an often breathless stream-of-consciousness.

We were rarely alone together. I was most always with Denise, whose name, I now realize, was in the front, middle, or end of nearly every sentence. "Oh, Denise, that outfit looks beautiful." "If you could stop by Walgreens, Denise, I could use a few things." "I have never thought that would happen. Did you, Denise?"

She was always saying Denise's name, even when Denise was not in the room. I suspect that is testimony to how important a person Denise was to her mother.

My mother-in-law rarely engaged me in a discussion that was not part exploratory. She was inquisitive and seemed to appreciate my opinion, nodding regularly and convincingly, but I suspect she was rarely in agreement. That is not to say that we disagreed at all. There were just a few topics that, with some delicate angling, I let float downstream rather than reel in.

Diane was a devoted fan of the *De Usuris* blog and of the *Conversations* podcast. I am not sure now that she ever listened to the podcasts, but I'd like to think that she did. Diane certainly read the features, and we talked about them from time to time when I called. Over the years, Denise and I enjoyed taking her mother to musicals, a performance of the Vienna Boys' Choir, or to watch her granddaughter evolve as a dancer in *The Nutcracker*.

I passed along several signed books for my mother-in-law on topics I thought she would enjoy. Denise helped organize big family birthday parties, which always involved a coordinated theme that Diane made a point of noticing. Those kinds of things always stood out. For her eightieth birthday a few years ago, puppet master Scott Gryder gave birth to "Puppet Diane," who wore a denim jacket and, in an accompanying video, danced to "I'm Happy."

When the family was around, Diane was particularly happy. She greeted everyone with that electric smile, or a warm hello over the phone. She loved her sisters—known collectively as "the Hertwig Girls"—who are also amazing women, mothers, and grandmothers. Good hardy stock, these are.

She was a single mother with six kids. She made sacrifices but admitted that, overall, the good far outweighed the bad. A few years ago, for Christmas—one of several favorite holidays she would celebrate with cards, decorations, and good cheer—Diane gave us a little sign that read, "Call your mother. She worries."

I am sure that mothers-in-law worry just as much as mothers do, and I am happy that I called from time to time just to say hello. I have no doubt that my extraordinary mother-in-law appreciated what everyone did for her along the way.

Most of all, I know deep down that Diane was devoted to the happiness and well-being of her entire family, and especially of her daughter and sons . . . and her "favorite" son-in-law.

Thanks, Mom.

APRIL 6, 2018

• DIANE MARIE (HERTWIG) MCGOWAN •
May 1, 1934—February 15, 2018

Act I, Scene 4

I wish there was a way to say this differently.
These talks are always hard; it's face-to-face.
The facts are clear that this will be a challenge.
You're both headed for a very unknown place.

Dr. Thompson
Act I, Scene 4

Lose the frown,
that's what my mother said.
He'll come around,
that's what my mother said.
Nothing's better than fried oysters on
a cold and rainy day.
Stand your ground, that's
what my mother said,
to me.

Katharine
Act 1, Scene 4

CHAPTER 16

ACT I, SCENE 4

SETTING: Dr. THOMPSON's Examination Room

SONGS: I WISH THERE WAS A WAY
            (TO SAY THIS DIFFERENTLY)

            WHAT'S A MOTHER TO DO

            WHAT MY MOTHER SAID

AT RISE: Scene changes to the examination room
            where THOMPSON reviews files and the
            CHIEF ADMINISTRATOR hovers over a
            financial spreadsheet.

The treatment center is insolvent and faces
challenges from a growing patient list, aging
facilities, declining insurance, and rising
operating expenses.

The situation is further complicated by THOMPSON's
insistence that all patients receive generous
discounts on treatments and, in many cases, no
charge at all. The discussion is familiar to the
partners, and there is friction on major issues.

The CHIEF has the last word.

                    CHIEF

     It's all business, Roy. Big business!

As the CHIEF exits, NURSE NAN escorts the TERONES
into the examination room.

THOMPSON tells TESS that her tests have come back
positive for genetic ovarian cancer. More tests
will be necessary to determine if TESS's sister
TOSS also has the gene.

THOMPSON and NAN sing I WISH THERE WAS A WAY (TO
SAY THIS DIFFERENTLY).

At the conclusion of the song, THOMPSON confronts
MOTHER, who admits that TESS and TOSS are not her
biological children, a fact not known to either of
them. In shock and disbelief, TESS and TOSS exit,
with THOMPSON following.

As the set revolves, MOTHER and KATHARINE console
each other.

MOTHER and KATHARINE sing the duet WHAT'S A MOTHER
TO DO? | WHAT MY MOTHER SAID.

                    LIGHTS FADE TO BLACK

CHAPTER 17

RULE ONE ALWAYS APPLIES

AFTER RETURNING HOME FROM the hospital, I spent almost four weeks watching the 2008 Summer Olympics and seven seasons of Magnum, P.I.

I confided in a small circle of friends, family, and work associates who were incredibly supportive and loving. Two of my best friends came to Chicago for visits during this period. One out-of-town media associate took time off to deliver lunch.

My daughter and granddaughter came, as well.

The company leadership and all of the staff in our organization did everything possible to cover the various operations and activities already underway at the library. Denise took care of our personal lives.

My mind was active and my days were full.

In mid-August, I was admitted to a clinic so doctors could insert a port-a-cath in my upper chest. This little device would allow direct access to a major artery for all treatments and blood tests. It also comes with the ultimate "chemo card"—as my daughter calls it—which only allows you special consideration when you fly on commercial air carriers.

A few days following the port-a-cath surgery, I became Denise's "Chemo Boy" and began a six-month, twelve-session chemotherapy treatment at Northwestern Hospital. No matter what perception you have about chemotherapy—whether from a member of your family or a close friend—no amount of information can prepare you for this treatment. The reason is Rule No. 3: Everyone's treatment is different. And shortly, I would learn Rule No. 4: Everyone reacts to cancer in a different way.

I have to explain, at this point, that once you tell anyone you have cancer, they will almost immediately recall someone they know who they feel has *exactly* what you have. If any of those people are reading this, they now know that I was only being polite when they spoke to me because, as a member, you can really only listen to anyone who is in "the Club"—those who have had cancer at any time in their life—or, for me, those who have had any amount of their colon removed in the last fifty years. Those people—and you know who you are—became instant soul mates. We are all in the same Club and have a mutual, indefinable respect and understanding that no one outside "the Club" can comprehend.

In truth, I have spoken to few people who have had chemotherapy. And each time, Rule No. 1 always applies.

CHAPTER 18

DEAR JOHN—REUNIONS

Dear John,

I've been thinking a lot recently about reunions.

Several thoughts came to me all of a sudden about these curious treks through our past. When you reach a certain age, you look backward and try to relive some of those experiences that may not now feel worth remembering. They do seem essential to understanding the person you have become. But, all too often, when you finally arrive at that wonderful place you're seeking, you find you may not have wanted to be there all along. It's painfully apparent to most of us that no one would really ever want to be eighteen again or even bring back memories from when you were—especially if you didn't have an exceptional time the first round.

I am thankful that I have many wonderful memories, but so many facets of my youth growing up in Vermont have been blocked by both age and the passage of time. It may be that our human ability to move beyond extremely painful moments works in our favor, if we allow it. I have only recently started to think about all these things and thought I'd write them down in a note to you.

My first significant high school reunion memory was my tenth high school reunion in my hometown in Northfield, Vermont. Arguably, we had a small turnout of ten or so, but it was great fun to see everyone at almost thirty years old. I recall that we looked so old and distinguished. I ran across a picture recently. I wore a tie and a sport coat. Most of my classmates had only seen me in worn jeans, T-shirts, and boots.

One classmate had a business, and another had three kids already. One had virtually not changed—and still has not—and others were already in the midst of redirecting their lives through a divorce. It might have had something to do with who dated whom, or who married whom, but members of our class who still lived in town never showed up for the reunion. So, our valiant group sought them out afterward. That's what you did in the early 1980s: if something needed attention, you attended to it.

I miss that attitude almost forty years later.

The reunion was held in the old mess hall at Norwich University in Northfield. Several generations of Northfield High School classes attended, all from the same year groups of sevens and twos. The emcee, a noted local attorney and alum, has always had a gift for eloquent public speaking. We joined together with several generations to sing our school song. No one ever knows the second verse. It was all quite surreal, in afterthought.

Twelve years later, I would attend my aunt's sixty-fifth high school reunion at NHS in the same hall—same wonderful emcee—but I was a guest. My aunt was aglow that night. It was there that her last existing classmate, Homer Denny—a legendary graduate and lifelong town resident—served up the most memorable opening line of any speech I have ever heard. Rising from his seat at our table to thunderous applause, he slowly crossed the large dance floor, stepped ever so carefully up the stairs to the stage, took the podium, and then, after several minutes adjusting his notes, the lamp, and his glasses, and settling into a now-silent room full of folks virtually sitting on the edges of their seats, he said, "Like the firefly who was caught up in the lawnmower . . . I am de-lighted . . . no-end . . . to be here!"

A memorable highlight for that reunion year was the two classmates dancing together. My aunt confessed that they never dated in school, as she was significantly taller than he was, and height mattered in those days. Still does when I'm dancing.

Over the years, it became important to me to stay connected with my high school and college classmates. Delving into your past often provides a sense of stability, regardless of how positive or negative the individual memories might be. So as I was thinking about that tenth reunion, and the people who still remain a part of my life, I realized that many other things were happening at the time. It was a family affair, since every year that I celebrated a reunion, one of my older brothers and my sister had their reunions, too. For a time, we all came back together.

It so happens that the year of my tenth reunion was a pivotal year in our family history. It may have been the last time that a group of sevens and twos alumni ever got together, as our class started doing our own thing in the years that followed. It was also, to the best of my knowledge, one of the last times that my older brother and sister joined their classmates at the same time.

That year, our time as a family at the farm that day is the most memorable part for me. What was happening to us, we would discover, was tearing our family apart.

Imagine a glorious late-spring day: blue sky, big puffy clouds, a newly mowed field, and trees bursting with the beauty of the Green Mountains. Most people in my town were not aware that a dark and difficult secret loomed in our family.

My mother had struggled with alcohol addiction for more than two decades.

Somehow, this was lost to nearly everyone around her. So, on that certain afternoon, leading up to our high school reunion, my family gathered in the kitchen of our old home on Roxbury Road. We had all but accepted what no one else knew about our mother and her hopeless addiction to alcohol. We ignored the problem as it grew worse every day. We enabled her and felt compelled to allow her to do and say what she wanted. And we consoled our father and minimized the high level of stress and low level of patience he had for the situation, not wanting to deal with the problem head-on. We were simply too self-absorbed in our own lives and the well-being of our own families or, to put it another way, torn between the love for our mother and trying to help her, and not knowing what to do.

Appeasing our father was a chore. He became more frustrated, despondent, and bitter about the situation—to the point that there was no light, laughter, or love in the house.

Coming home had become a burden.

That morning would change all our lives forever. I distinctly remember discussing the situation with my father as he went off to work and my brother looked on. The murmur would spread to my sister later that morning when she arrived. At lunchtime, in the middle of a beautiful day with her family, my mother was incomprehensible. It was quiet. Once again we were trapped in a dark room with the sun shining brightly outside.

Without a word, my brother, showing great strength and love, confronted my mother directly in front of the entire family. Nothing like that had ever happened before. The house shook. He stormed into my parent's bedroom, ripped out the fifth of vodka hidden under the mattress, and then poured it down the kitchen sink. His frustration and anger were uncontrollable. Rage filled him, and he stormed outside and threw the bottle out onto the hillside beyond our farmhouse, deep into the grove of trees planted there. All the while, my mother pleaded with him to stop being angry, to help her kill the pain, and to give her just one drop from the bottle.

That day, my brother became a compassionate anchor for my mother and for the entire family. He sat quietly with her for an hour and told her that she needed to face her addiction, find help and let us help her through. He pledged to her that he would do everything he could to make her pain go away. We all thought she might have heard him that day, but it was hard to tell from her body language and from the years of torture she brought upon herself through alcoholism. She was distraught, hurt, shaking, and sad.

We all went to our reunion that night and talked amongst ourselves about what the next step should be. My brother took the lead locally: he found a social worker and developed a plan for the family that ultimately led to my mother admitting herself into a three-month program to deal with her addiction. That started a glorious seven-year period that would ultimately ensure that she and my father could spend some of their twilight years together truly in love. It was a long and painful recovery, but my mother took much pride in her sobriety during that period. Her strength of purpose, conviction, and unconditional love was renewed.

There are sometimes darker sides to these reunion stories. And even though I'd like to think things always turn out well, they don't. As I reflect on the reunions I've had in my life, they all seem to be wrapped in other challenging situations. One story for another day would be my thirty-fifth high school reunion, which, after months of great planning on my part, would not include me at all because my daughter was admitted to the emergency room midway through her pregnancy. She gave birth prematurely to my beautiful, miracle granddaughter.

Reconnecting can also be bittersweet. Our college reunion brought together more than 100 theater students from thirty class years to honor our college mentors a couple of years ago. That high point will always be associated with the passing of both men during the planning process and my diagnosis of stage 3C colon cancer that followed a few days after returning to Chicago. I chose not to stay in touch immediately following that event until I knew that things would be much better. They are, I am very happy to say.

Maybe all we are looking for is to be loved again by those we admired so long ago—those who were closest to us, or perhaps more importantly, those who we could not love at the time.

That time so long ago is documented well in my family. Unknown to the rest of us, my mother wrote my brother quite eloquently a few years later. It was hard for me to read that letter after the first time we heard it during her funeral, but it is brilliantly succinct and profound—a powerful work of prose.

Recently, I asked my brother for a copy of that letter so that I could relive this experience one more time. It now brings a great deal of comfort to me to know that, years later, my mother could describe the events and feelings she had at that moment, even though we thought, at the time, that she might not be anywhere in the room. Surprising still that she could articulate with such beauty and grace how she felt when she saw the glint of glass on the hillside on another beautiful late-spring day in Vermont and realized that it was the empty bottle of vodka that my brother had thrown so long ago.

I make a point as often as I can these days to tell the people close to me how much I love them and how much they mean to me. I think it is important that they know, even if it doesn't sound like just the right thing to say at the time. You have, dear sir, taught me to get it out, speak up, and tell people how I feel. The love you share in your short notes and messages, and indeed all you do, always makes me smile.

Just a couple of things I thought I'd let you know today. In truth, we are not so dissimilar in these life experiences. Our challenge always is to keep people focused forward, learning and enjoying life, and taking a moment to thank those who show us so much love, even when they might not be in the room.

JULY 15, 2009

CHAPTER 19

PEOPLE I KNEW— GEORGE TURNER

I WANTED TO REMEMBER every detail of the conversation as it might have happened thirty-two years ago, or twenty years later . . . or just last week. There are many indescribable moments that, when all summed, create a vivid tapestry of life. This was one of those and only became more significant, and poignant, as reality settled in—all of it captured in a worn, weathered memoir of Vietnam from the shelf of a dear, passed friend.

While we all leave parts of ourselves with others, there is an unimaginable quality to this story—but it is absolute fact.

It evolved around the memory and passion of a professor who treasured what being alive offers a human being. He lived each day with a deep respect for history, served his country in uniform—in peace and in war—and placed literature and the written word in a revered and sacred place for his students and all who knew him.

The author of perhaps the most significant memoir ever written about the Vietnam era plays an unsuspecting role in this story. How these two men's lives intersected, not once but four times, is the heart of this tale. We are just now recognizing the meaning and purpose those encounters provided.

For Phil Caputo, the story begins in 1964, but for George Turner, it began in 1944 off the coast of Italy. Each served in combat in very different wars with very different outcomes.

Caputo would publish *A Rumor of War* in 1977. George Turner would recognize its significance to the university he had served for nearly two decades before he finished Caputo's dedication. Walt Levy was Caputo's grad-school classmate and a central character in the greater story—and one of the two men to whom the book is dedicated. Levy was Turner's student in 1959.

First Lieutenant Walter Neville Levy was also the first graduate of Norwich University to die in Vietnam.

So it was a key story for George Turner to tell his students, through the study of Caputo's brilliant narrative of the futility of war and the anguish of command in Vietnam. He lectured regularly on the topic, compelling his students to understand the significance of service in combat and the different lessons of the Vietnam War through Caputo's work.

And over the course of the next decade, when Norwich planned a military writers' program, Turner made it clear that the event would be of no value to anyone unless Caputo came to discuss Vietnam with former director of Central Intelligence William E. Colby.

Turner and Caputo had never met.

Armed with little information, I was surprised to not only get in touch with Caputo by phone, but also to offer and confirm his attendance in a matter of days, despite his having no prior knowledge of the importance of the Levy legacy to Norwich.

Turner was elated. He would be able to connect with a writer he respected beyond measure. Caputo had no idea what was in store.

He arrived at Norwich in April 1996, well aware now of the deep connection between his friendship with Levy and the school. He met students, attended classes, and, over a two-day period, participated in three panels with Colby—introducing the inaugural panel with a brilliant essay about the costs of war. It was a powerful session, described as a "unique collection of experts" to include Colby, Caputo, W. E. B. Griffin, Carlo D'Este, Harry Coyle, and Cole Kingseed.

That evening, Caputo was the keynote speaker, and we all told him what we knew about Walt Levy. Turner smiled from the front-center table. As Caputo spoke of the young Marine who gave his life in an attempt to save an already-lost comrade, he talked around the Norwich motto without ever mentioning the words: "I Will Try."

There is a wonderful irony in life: the brilliance of a memoir that so ably captures the horror of war; the connection of a student and professor and lifelong friends. As I visited with George's widow last weekend, I recalled my early-morning wake-up call to Caputo; how his participation galvanized the first session of the writers' symposium that was subsequently named for Colby, and how significant it was that Colby and Levy were connected on "the Hill."

Later the next day, Ann said she had found something in George's room I might like to see. It was a weathered, well-read, and heavily annotated 1977 paperback edition of *A Rumor of War* with the initials "GRT" on the cover in blue and his "G. R. Turner" signature in red on the first facing pages. He had stuffed in its pages the original front-page article about the first public session of the symposium; and a pocket card from the April 11–12, 1996, program with "Phoenix Program" notated in blue under Colby's bio. There were three copies of the obituary Turner wrote that had been published in the Norwich Record about his former student who had become the first Norwich casualty of the Vietnam War—two in the front of the book and one with a plain white notecard inserted at page 208, where Levy's story is retold. There is a professor's notation at the bottom of the page, indicating that the chapter and page references differ in the new edition of the book. There was a *Publisher's Weekly* review of Caputo's 1996 book *Equation for Evil* with a thorough interview about his career. And perhaps best of all: two sets of the professor's quiz questions and answers—from different eras—about virtually every major theme in Caputo's book.

Written with great care, there was an inscription under Matthew 24:6–13:

April 10, 1996
To George Turner, who also knew Walt & of his virtues.
Best wishes to a great teacher,
Philip Caputo

"I think," Ann told me that day, "he would want you to have this."

There are many indescribable moments that, when all summed, create a vivid tapestry of life. This was one of those, and it only became more significant and poignant as reality settled in.

One final lesson in life from the professor to a grateful student.

OCTOBER 15, 2009

CHAPTER 20

PROFESSIONAL COUNSELING

THE FOLLOWING LETTER WAS never read by my therapist. My letter was among other mail found by her partner in her office when he began the process of making calls to advise clients that she had passed away, alone in her apartment, sometime over the previous weekend. Her death was not discovered right away, nor reported widely, and it took me a couple days to get back to her business partner. Realizing that I had been writing my letter to her during her final hours was what my friend Roger Ebert would have called one of the several "coincidences" that occur in life.

In addition to providing the sad news, her partner told me there were steps underway to take charge of her many recent patients, of which I was one. I told her partner, and Dr. Lloyd knew, that I would be taking a break for several weeks, or perhaps longer, to sort through the things we had discussed following our last session. I had no further sessions scheduled.

Writing this letter was one of the most important psychological events I'd had since before my cancer diagnosis. It was a breakthrough. I was excited to tell her about my discovery and to thank her for her insightful support. I asked her partner to open the envelope, read the letter, take out the invoice and payment, and send the original letter and envelope back to me, which he did.

I had started writing on Friday evening, April 9, after seeing a screening and discussion at the Gene Siskel Film Center of Howard Reich's film *Prisoner of Her Past*, the harrowing story of his mother's flight from the Nazis during World War II and her struggle with late-onset post-traumatic stress disorder. I revised my letter on Saturday, April 10, and sent it off that day. I was quite single-minded about the whole thing, Denise will recall. It was certainly meant to be a sincere thank-you and "so long for now," as I felt that it was not only validation of our short-but-intense professional relationship, but also a positive step to let her know that the time we had spent had been productive, healing, and appreciated.

Over time, I have come to realize that people come into our lives for a reason, and it is often our challenge to understand what that reason is. Dr. Lloyd's last act of kindness, during our final session, was to handwrite a name and phone number on a card, which allowed me entrée to an exceptional physician who ultimately solved a multitude of medical and emotional problems. I am happy with my new "quarterback": a key player on a cancer "veteran's" medical team, according to Dr. Lloyd.

I recounted this story one Monday night in Booth #23—the Gene Siskel booth—at Petterino's with two other members of "the Club," who were coping with their complex issues with high degrees of courage and compassion. I'm convinced that the more in tune we are with ourselves, the more able we are to read these situations in real time, without the benefit—or need—of reflection.

This will always be the case when I think of my movie night with Howard Reich at the Siskel, or of the extraordinary enthusiasm I discovered when I realized I had to get back to writing things down on a regular basis—something I enjoy now more than ever.

John Callaway told me once that writing is how we deal with stress and grief.

I was pleased that I was able to tell Dr. Lloyd how grateful I was for her help, understanding, and kindness. I am equally content that at the moment of passing, we may all be connected by a prescient force that compels us to see things with greater clarity and more sensitivity.

When I tell this story, which is not often, I always remember a little more about our sessions together. Those memories provide more strength for every day ahead—which was probably her plan all along.

CHAPTER 21

PEOPLE I KNEW— DR. EDITH LLOYD

Dear Dr. Lloyd,

I had a bit of a revelation recently that I thought I would write to you about.

I have taken many positive steps in the last few months. Your care and attention have been the guiding light that has shown the way. I will be taking more of those steps in the days and weeks ahead, thanks to you.

Back to the revelation: Although I had seen three or four versions and read the book, a thought occurred to me last night at the premiere viewing of my good friend Howard Reich's new film, *Prisoner of Her Past*—a documentary our foundation helped fund. It was dedicated to our mutual friend and mentor, the late John Callaway, and all about Howard's mother's late-onset PTSD stemming from her horrific World War II adolescent experience—much of which still remains a haunting mystery.

We have talked a little at our sessions about PTSD from the post-cancer and patient-care perspective. I felt that I was closing in on that being at the center of the crisis occurring late last year in my life. Howard's discovery of his mother's trauma, along with relating the experience to PTSD cases in child victims of the Katrina disaster, has always been an enlightening part of the story. This project has been developing since Howard and I met in 2003, so I had forgotten a lot along the way, as my attention span has been focused in other areas.

All this is not, however, at the core of my revelation; only preamble.

It happened during the post-film discussion, inspired by a friend of mine I invited who was in Chicago on business this week. Catherine never expected that Denise and I would treat her to a film at the Siskel Film Center during her visit. She uniquely understands the culture of independent filmmaking, has knowledge of the topic, and asked, for me, the most salient question of the night: was Howard's mother's PTSD experience "triggered" by a memory, incident, or anniversary? Howard noted that the answer is in his book, which I had read long ago, but *not* in the film. In his mother's case, the night she ran away frightened from her house in Skokie was ten years to the day after Howard's father, also a child Holocaust survivor, had died.

We have talked about many issues in my business and personal life, but I do not recall discussing that the twentieth anniversary of my mother's passing was December 15, 2009, although I am convinced now that we must have. Each year over the last two decades, I have intellectualized it somehow—understanding how I felt, how it affected my father and my young family, and how we soldiered on through the holidays that year for everyone else in the family.

This past year, I thought about it daily for months in advance. In retrospect, I refused to talk about it or even realize it at the time. With all the various factors at play, I came apart emotionally in early December. On that day, after weeks of urging from Denise, I called Dr. Morgan. That was the day he suggested I call you—the day my life started moving forward again.

While researching combat stories, and during the interviews at the library, I am continually fascinated by the resilience of the human body, mind, and spirit to endure. When I compared combat PTSD to my life, a January 2010 counseling session hardly seemed necessary. Fortunately, I went forward. There is no way that I would have been able to start to put any of the pieces together alone. I would still be wondering, frustrated, and in denial; kicking the can down the road rather than envisioning myself "as thin." Nothing's perfect, but it's been a really great start. This is the first bit of personal writing since the patient-care letter—a turning point to be sure.

I had another long talk with Dr. Morgan last weekend, and it was much more upbeat than the one in December. He is a big Edith Lloyd fan and is very much in agreement with our plan to proceed with new primary care. We will also work to have the port-a-cath removed in the next three to four weeks, and he told me about a significant new program at Northwestern to fund holistic approaches to evaluating post-cancer symptoms in patients.

We also discussed how patients naturally move among different physicians and specialists for a host of reasons. I understand now more clearly from you that it is not a separation or divorce, but simply steps along the way to gather more information, make the best decision, solve a problem, or just talk. That's what Dr. Morgan told me the first time I called him in early December. I have deeply enjoyed our conversations over the past few months. Perhaps, the next time we meet, I can learn a little bit more about you.

Thank you for your patience, for listening, for your expert advice, and for helping me through this extremely confusing and challenging period of my life. I will not forget your kindness.

APRIL 10, 2010

CHAPTER 22

IMERMAN ANGELS— A CONVERSATION WITH BEN BORNSTEIN

PERHAPS YOU MET JONNY Imerman when he roamed the halls of a cancer center in 2003, thankful to be alive and receiving treatment for testicular cancer. He struggled with a life-changing diagnosis, like every other patient. And he was surrounded by family and friends who provided support and encouragement.

You might have been one of the other patients who faced all of these same life challenges, but still felt alone—without a close-knit support system or anyone available who was your own age or who had faced the same diagnosis and treatment you faced.

Jonny's isolation in the middle of a busy cancer treatment center, as well as a series of conversations with other patients, inspired him and co-founder John May to establish Imerman Angels, a Chicago-based nonprofit that brings together people dealing with cancer with mentor angels—or someone of a similar age who has fought the same type of cancer.

According to CEO Ben Bornstein, since 2006, Imerman Angels has expanded operations to fifty states and sixty countries and has made more than 34,000 connections with the support of 8,000 mentor angels matching up a staggering 137 types of cancer.

In our wide-ranging conversation on August 8, 2017, Bornstein, a three-time cancer survivor himself, discussed the extraordinary impact of program innovations in patient aftercare and what's ahead for an organization that is changing the outlook for cancer patients, one survivor at a time.

BB: Nowadays, we're quite fortunate that survival rates are as high as they are for many types of cancer. It's not a death sentence anymore. It's certainly true that some people don't make it through their cancer fight despite their hard work and efforts, and the great medical care they might get. Many folks are now survivors that wouldn't have been twenty, thirty years, or even ten years ago. To the question of timing, cancer affects you differently depending on where you are in the rest of your life. If you think about the human experience, it's a confluence of all the things at once, and for most people, if it hits you as an adult, it's disruptive to your family life and it's disruptive to your professional life. If it hits as a kid, it all of a sudden brands you as "different": You're now on chemo instead of going to tennis practice or baseball practice. And so all of that is quite impactful.

Now, on the medical side, they've made incredible strides forward in the medicine available: The surgical techniques, not just for cancer, but most types of medical treatment, are so much better— less invasive, faster recovery times with great countermeasure drugs, if you will, for nausea and some of the side effects from chemotherapy that make it more tolerable than it once was. Still not a walk in the park, mind you, but more tolerable than it once was.

So, I think the medical advances have been tremendous in the last thirty years in contrast to the psychosocial support resources available to cancer fighters, which had not evolved quite as quickly. Imerman Angels is providing that missing link of a mentoring experience, a like-to-like experience to a cancer fighter or a caregiver who is going through great emotional distress and trauma with that mentor angel who has been through it before and can help guide you, if you will, through your tough experience and help you emerge on the back end as positively as you can.

ET: And we've also come to a point in time, medically, where people are understanding that it runs in the family and that we've dealt with this before. In my particular case, I have a lot of cancer in my past, but none of it was identified as colon cancer, which was my cancer. And so I didn't seek early screening for colon cancer. How important is it for people to understand the health legacy they have in their family? And how can they use that information to guide their own medical decisions in the future?

BB: There is no doubt that there is a genetic component to cancer as you describe it with your own family, and as I have with my family. Lots of cancer in the family. So, for me, I'm always particularly sensitive to any unusual feelings of fatigue and, more obvious, finding blood in your stool—things like that. Any lumps or anything that doesn't heal as quickly as you would think. My second cancer was a tongue cancer. I was a non-tobacco chewing young adult and not a heavy drinker. My dentist discovered a little flap of skin in a spot in the back of my tongue and that's how we found it.

Whether you had a genetic history or not, if you're seeing the actual growth of something, you take care of it right away. And one thing we always emphasize at Imerman Angels is be sure to be in touch with your body. Don't be afraid of going to the doctor. Many young adults, in particular, are the most reluctant group. Men, in particular, were a little more stubborn, I suppose, to go in, to see and gain that medical advice and medical help, but it can make the difference between surviving and not making it through your cancer journey to find things early. Early detection for cancer, like most medical conditions, is the name of the game for survival.

ET: One of the lessons that we learned from Jonny Imerman is to remain positive. I'm told he's one of the most positive people you'll ever meet—exciting and encouraging to people to keep going, to keep fighting. Tell us a little bit about Jonny and about the positive-attitude factor in all of this.

BB: Jonny Imerman launched Imerman Angels eleven years ago. And it was really premised on the belief, in his own experience, that everybody needs something more than just the medical care and just the positive relationship and support from family and friends. What he brings to the table is that extra element of "never give up the fight," positive energy, always thinking toward making it to the other end of your cancer journey, and then doing a great job of transmitting his own energy into the organization.

We now call upon Imerman Angels, this army of 8,000 who are survivors of cancer, to mentor and give back to those going through a similar journey themselves at this time. I would say, culturally, that's been a big part of the footprint of Imerman Angels. Cancer is an equalizer. Cancer humbles you. We can stay positive and still try to have some fun and be a little bit laid-back as a culture here, as we're helping people deal with something very serious when your life is on the line through a cancer diagnosis.

ET: And this is a very big number: 8,000 volunteers. Give me a sense of what kind of an impact they are making to this very universal disease.

BB: We have 8,000 mentor angels as volunteers. No one's paid within the matchup at Imerman Angels, and it's always a free service that we offer to the cancer fighters. The 8,000 mentor angels can have multiple mentees. So we have 34,000-plus who are involved in connections all around the world in sixty countries and now in all fifty states. Our headquarters are here in Chicago, and then we have a big presence in New York, Los Angeles, and Detroit.

The impact can go a lot of different directions. Remember, this is a human connection. It's a human relationship between two people. We train our mentor angels, but we then are not recording or monitoring the interactions. It takes on the personalities, if you will, of the two people involved. So sometimes that means there'll be encouragement to get a second opinion or to check out a clinical trial for a tough-to-beat cancer like stomach cancer or glioblastoma diagnosis. And in those cases, this matchup can really be a lifesaver because it may take somebody who is a bit down, a bit depressed about things and is only getting one set of information from one medical professional. And the experience of our mentor angel may encourage them to receive a broader set of information that is available to them and can save a life.

We have also had situations where folks are feeling quite down and distressed about their cancer experience and our matchups help with that depression. Somebody could be, "Geez, do I want to keep pushing it all?" Our mentor angels help push them through that, and we have a vast array of testimonials of folks among this mentor-angel population who have really encouraged and helped and played a vital role in the cancer journey of that fighter.

ET: The mentors are all basically the same age or about the same age. They are trying to be matched that way with the same cancer. And when I was going through this, I recognized that a lot of friends of mine were trying to relate to me saying, "Oh, I have a cousin who has had what you have." I had colon cancer, and they said, "Well, he had brain cancer." I said, "Well, they're different." Everyone's different. Everyone having cancer in a different age group is different. So how important is it to match those people age-wise and to their own specific cancer diagnosis?

BB: Tremendously important. We call it a "connection perfection" mentality. If you think about the back end of this, it's essentially a database with all these different fields. And we score them the way we think is most important, and then we add a human overlay on top of it through our call center, so that a patient and a fighter can tell us, "For me, this is the most important. I really want somebody with the same religious background because our religion doesn't allow for certain types of treatment," or, "I'd really like to have somebody who's also in Chicago"—or if they're in Chicago and really want somebody in California. We match up folks across sixty countries. Sometimes they want fellow countrymen or women to be matched up there.

We are not constrained by HIPAA as it is all self-disclosed information, and we capture a lot of data—everything from name, date of birth, address, sexual orientation, religion—anything somebody wants to tell. If you have a military background and you want to talk to a fellow veteran going through a cancer experience, we can match up to that factor as well. So we try to make it as like-for-like as possible and what's important to them. For example, my mother was a caregiver to me as a childhood cancer fighter. She was a caregiver mentor angel, and she has matched up with other mothers who have kids going through cancer. It is less important to allow those mothers their mentor angel in the same geography. It is more important that they are facing the same experience. How do you deal with that? How do you fight through that? It really depends on the circumstances, and we want the fighter and the user of our services to have an active role in defining that relationship.

ET: Let's talk a little bit about the caregiver of the cancer fighter. My wife—she was actually my girlfriend, then became my wife during this period—would say to people that a lot of times, people are very focused on the cancer fighter, but not so much on the caregiver. How does the relationship between the mentor help to ease or promote a better understanding of what the family is going through for the friends and family of the fighters?

BB: Many of us have been in that situation with a loved one going through a terrible illness, whether it's cancer or something else. So one of the insights Jonny Imerman had early on in founding Imerman Angels was that the caregiver will be just as important a part of the cancer journey that we have described as the fighter themselves, in many cases. And sometimes, emotionally, it's even tougher on a caregiver because they're not in the middle of the fight. Sometimes it's always easier if you're in the game to affect the game, right? And so for the caregivers—a spouse, a parent to a child, a brother or sister of a cancer fighter—we match those folks up to somebody—again, a like-for-like experience—who has been caregiving to somebody with the same cancer type, at the same age, with the same relationship.

To find parents of kids going through cancer is the biggest category we have of those caregiver mentor angels. But sometimes it's a very tough cancer to beat. It's glioblastoma and a fighter's spouse where the fighter may not make it. And we do offer bereavement matches that continue on past the time of a particular fighter's journey ending.

ET: Let's talk a little bit about the long-term of fighting cancer. There are some great stories—I've read a lot of them here at Imerman—great testimonials about what you have done for patients through positive reinforcement. Cancer is a tricky thing. You have dealt with it three times. Give us an idea of this journey for you. Not just as a kid, but then later and now . . . every day when you are moving through your life.

BB: I would say, for me, it's been interesting because I've had cancer at three fairly well-defined times of life. I had it fourteen years old as a kid; twenty-eight years old as a young adult, unmarried professional; and then forty-two years old as a married guy and thinking about starting a family and all of that. And oddly (I'm a numbers guy at heart—before I was full-time at Imerman Angels, I was a Wall Street guy) it was every fourteen years. So, I say to people, when I'm fifty-six years old, that next fourteen-year mark may be a very nervous year for me.

To your question, how do I think about it? I guess several things come to mind. The first, being very mindful without it impacting my life and being paranoid about health. I'm very mindful of my health. I'm aware of my health. I'm not fearful going to doctors for checkups. I try to edge a little bit more toward a test than not doing a test, doing a diagnostic versus not doing a diagnostic, because I know, as we said earlier, if you catch a cancer earlier, the chances for survival are dramatically better and the experience is so much more rough once you have something, and you have to go through that treatment, than getting a blood test or a bone scan or something along those lines.

When I was fourteen, I was in a baseball game, in my stance, and got hit by a pitch directly on what turned out to be a metastasized tumor: non-Hodgkin's lymphoma.

So, some spiritual higher power or whatever you want to call it, whether you're religious or not, something was looking out for me the day that I got hit by a pitch directly on a tumor site that otherwise I wouldn't have known about that allowed the medical team to diagnose the cancer early, which probably without that, I might not be here today. So it's that kind of thinking. You have to be on top of it. You have to be early and just be aware.

And at the end of the day, you can't spend your life worrying about everything. You get in a car. You cross the street. Things can happen. You have heart attacks or sudden medical problems at any given moment. You can't worry about it on the constant, but on the other hand, you can't ignore it. So that balance is important.

I encourage folks to tilt a little bit more toward being aware of their bodies, what's going on. Feeling a little different? Make sure you see a doctor—those kinds of things, because the detection technology today is so much superior to what it was in 1985, when I had my first cancer, and 1999, when I had my second cancer. It can really make the difference between making it and not making it. And then, fortunately, you have resources now today with Imerman Angels being as large as it is—34,000 connected through 2016. We have 137 cancer types in our database. There is no other organization that has that kind of data, which is why you find world-class institutions—Mayo, MD Anderson, Sloan Kettering, as well as Northwestern, UIC and others in Chicago—referring patients to us, because as large as they are and as accessible as they are with their medical expertise, they don't have as much data as we have about cancer fighters.

ET: And when you are going through this, did you—or do you—practice any kinds of coping mechanisms? Do you do something positively for yourself to get you through those times when you are thinking a little bit more about it than you should be?

BB: An excellent question. There are a couple of different things I do that I think help. I certainly hit the gym with some regularity. That's one. Just trying to stay at some level of physical health. I don't do any formal meditation, but I do take time every day to think about the day. Think about the world. Try to have some direction to it. And I guess I would say the most important thing is you do become incredibly self-reliant in some ways, when you go through something like a cancer journey. So it does empower you, if you will, to be your own person. To put things in a professional context, or a personal life context, in perspective when you've gone through something that's life threatening. I hadn't had the military background that you described that you've had in your history. And I'm imagining maybe something a little bit similar there, too, where you're going through something that's so difficult and your life is on the line that it changes you on the back end. And probably, when you do get to the back end, makes you a better and stronger person.

ET: I want to clarify that I am not a military veteran myself, but I have told a lot of military stories of combat from over forty Medal of Honor recipients and other veterans. It was a life-changing experience for me to see their strength. Along the way, I made a correlation between combat and cancer, particularly the depression and the post-traumatic stress that results. How does a cancer family group coalesce around the concept that post-traumatic stress is a real thing for cancer fighters—recognizing the need to seek treatment for it and using other techniques?

BB: The evidence that we have seen reported in journals is that almost 90 percent of folks going through a cancer fight experienced emotional distress, and, almost universally, those folks say that having alleviation of that stress would make a significant difference to their quality of life in their cancer journey. From our end, we emphasize to our mentor angels that you are not there to play doctor or provide medical advice, per se. So when the cancer journey gets to the point where a therapist, a psychiatrist, or a mental health professional is warranted, we do encourage our matchups, our mentoring angels, to point that out to fighters. And we also, somewhat frequently, have folks call in who we realize, through our in-house expertise in our call center, may need a mental health professional to step in first.

And sometimes, it's both: they need us and they need a little more. In my own experience, most hospitals and medical centers do a decent job of providing a social-work support system, as well as the kind of individual mentor that we provide. And those folks are quite good at assessing the situation, then suggesting that you may need a therapist, this treatment experience, or maybe you need to see a psychiatrist. Maybe you need drugs to help with some depression. That's not our job to make that call, but we certainly have some expertise in seeing so many fighters and knowing when it might be warranted to consider such an approach.

ET: It's not unhealthy to seek out that advice and concede to taking these drugs. There are some drugs out there that can really help you out.

BB: I'd say that's a hundred percent right. I think it really depends on the person, as to how they are going to react to a cancer diagnosis, but it is quite traumatic, and many folks could use some help along the way. And it's appropriate in those contexts.

ET: What do you say to groups that want to do things for people? They want to reach out. People want to be a part and help out a lot of times. And I can tell you from my own experience, and maybe you had the same thing, there are a lot of times that I don't want to have a lot of people around. There are times when I'll be out there, and I understand what my place is, but other times I just wanted to kind of be back in the background and not talk to anybody. How do you approach these groups of people who want to be part of the solution, and how do you channel that into a positive result for the family?

BB: We tend to find our fighters and our mentor angels in sort of three distinct channels. The first is quite obviously, I suppose, the medical centers in the medical environment. So that's nurse navigators, social workers, oncologists, informational tables that we set up at hospitals and facilities in our major hub cities, where we'll find these fighters and build our team that way.

The second way, which may be a little less obvious because this is free and cancer affects almost everybody, we have a version of a corporate road show where we talk to companies like McDonald's and Boeing—both local Chicago companies—offering a great resource for free to their employee base. And it is not just employees, but their extended families and their friends who need Imerman Angels mentoring services. We stay in touch with a lot of big companies and find more fighters and find the subset of the population that could make use of the service we provide them.

One of the things we hear most frequently still among our mentor angels is, "I wish I had known about this service when I was going through my own journey." And that gives us a confidence and some validation that what we're offering people is of great value. And if more cancer fighters knew about this, they would use it. As proud as we are to have these 34,000 matchups since inception at a run rate of about 3,000 connected per year, there are millions that are going through cancer journeys. And so we're just scratching the surface, even as a market leader.

The other thing we've discovered is you have to think about different communities that you're working with. We have a big outreach program to Spanish-speaking communities. We have all of our literature and our website in Spanish as well as English, and there's different techniques and different styles and different approaches that sometimes work better in those communities. The first question is often, "Does somebody on the Imerman Angels team speak Spanish?" and we do have two bilingual professionals among our team.

Similarly, within the African American community, there are different ways to seek out support. We try to know where are and who are we working with. We do that through an ambassador program: volunteers who work with us in cities all around the country who have a better sense of how that particular geography may collaborate with our office.

ET: And it's all worked out of this relatively modest office here in Chicago. It's pretty amazing what you do on a daily, a monthly, and an annual basis to help put all these people together.

BB: We appreciate the opportunity to tell our story. The goal that Jonny had when he started this was, "Nobody should have to face cancer alone." So we want to make sure that everybody has the opportunity to make that decision for themselves, and if they decide to use our services, they can.

www.imerman.org
AUGUST 8, 2017

Act I, Scene 5

Don't be blue.
You're in the blue room.
It's routine. Quite commonplace,
And you'll get used to the pace
Of spending hours in the blue room,
So don't be blue.

Joe Gorilla
Act I, Scene 5

CHAPTER 23

ACT I, SCENE 5

SETTING: Chemotherapy Treatment Room

SONG: JUST A DAY IN THE BLUE ROOM

AT RISE: In the treatment room, patients fill all six blue chairs. The IMPATIENT PATIENT is in the wheelchair with the ORDERLY nearby. The patients are in the middle of their treatment.

JOE, dressed as an attendant, and the CHAOSALS are nearby. The CHAOSALS raise havoc (moving paper supplies from the storage cabinet to the refrigerator, taking coats off hangers as patients hang them, locking the bathroom door from the inside) and other business.

JOE sings JUST A DAY IN THE BLUE ROOM. The song culminates with a full-cast dance number with patients vying for the bathroom as they roll IV stands around.

The number ends with everyone back in their chairs, exhausted and weary.

BLACKOUT

CHAPTER 24

EATING APPLESAUCE WITH A KNIFE

Treatment Seven of Ten

I AM IN THE middle of my seventh treatment, secure with my pump blasting chemotherapy through my veins and coming off two normal days, thanks to steroids. The middle days of the two weeks between treatments grow longer. I have little or no energy to do anything on these days.

Unfortunately, obligations that do not involve golf still come along during these periods, and, usually, with a large amount of determination, I rise to the occasion. After losing all the weight, everyone says I look great. That's comforting, because I work hard to maintain any weight, to drink fluids, and to keep my system regulated—a tall order with all the drugs I am processing.

And then Monday comes, and life goes back to normal— well, almost.

Because there are some things that all of us in "the Club" have to deal with—sensitivity to touching anything cold, the ringing of neuropathy in hands and feet, drinking or eating anything cold, and the uncanny metallic taste caused by metal silverware—nothing is normal.

Early on, I started carrying around one of those plastic to-go settings and a healthy supply of applesauce, my new favorite snack. The single servings are warm from hanging out in my satchel, and I bring three or four with me on a "normal" day. Of course, I eat the first one with the spoon, and, after throwing away that plastic utensil, realize I must eat the next serving with the fork. Not to be under-challenged, I never learn my lesson, and I throw away the fork. By the time I try to eat my applesauce with a knife, I'm down to primitively sucking the applesauce out of the plastic cup.

I shared this story with my friends, and one thoughtful soul gave me a set of wooden flatware. Now the challenge is to remember to bring it along whenever I go out. Denise scoured Amazon a few weeks later and located a hand-carved set that has made life easier. If you know someone in "the Club," it is the perfect present.

NOVEMBER 2008

CHAPTER 25

MAKING HAY—THOUGHTS ON FATHER'S DAY

FATHER'S DAY IS ONE of those special days each year. Our fathers teach us so many wonderful things we take for granted that it is hard to sort one from the other, until the years have passed, and we reflect on what happened along the way. I love and respect all those I have come to think are just like a father to me. But the fact is, on Father's Day, my thoughts go back to the man himself.

After my parents married, they built a small house across from my paternal grandparents' home on Roxbury Road in Northfield, Vermont. By the time the two older boys were beginning to walk, the project had been completed. It was a small three-bedroom house with a den and two modest bedrooms off each side in the back. We had a natural spring for water and no central heat in the back section. The oversized wood furnace in the basement provided sufficient heat for the entire house if we left the door to the den open at night. Someone opened the door every morning at 5 a.m., after lighting a new fire. And we had plenty of blankets. But often, massive snowstorms rolled in and buried our humble home.

On those mornings, the tile floor showed signs of frost.

Perhaps my earliest memory is my mother waking me as I slept in the top drawer of an old white dresser we had in the boys' room in our house. That's not where I usually slept. I was repositioned that night, and several others, to make room for younger visitors who occupied my crib in the den. The other members of the visiting family would huddle up in my sister's room or across the road at my grandparents' house. We always accommodated visitors in our home.

I am the youngest in my generation. Ten and eleven years separate me from my brothers, and five came between my sister and me. As I came of age in understanding, my brothers were already in junior high school, and my sister had acquired a vast group of rural girlfriends who would spend weekends and overnights at our house. I was the disruptive little brother in the late '50s—a time important for your dad's car and a radio. Vermont teens could only imagine where Wolfman Jack, the Four Seasons, and other musical groups came from far outside the Green Mountains of our beautiful state.

My father was always careful about ensuring that I was mentored properly through the unique group of older children, relatives, youthful hormones, and athletic obstacles that can be placed in the way of a young lad on a farm. While my brothers worked with my father on the farm chores or played sports in school, Dad always made sure I paid attention, listened, and heard his opinion on any proceedings. That I was too young to participate didn't matter. I was included, and that's all that counted.

The boys split the duties in my family. They'll argue about which one did more or less, so I won't pass judgment on that point here. They did take me on walks to herd the cows home in the evening, let me tag along to ride high on the hay wagon in the summertime, and made sure I was outside with my small plastic shovel and bright-red snowsuit, trying to make some mark in the mountains of snow that collected on our lawn every winter.

My grandfather was a source of great curiosity to me. He lived in that old house directly across the road from ours, and people tell me I followed him everywhere. Each week, when we had finished a new box of Kellogg's Corn Flakes, my mother would help me tear off the back of the box, and I would scurry to my grandmother's kitchen. There, with these massive seamstress scissors of hers, she would carefully cut out the image along the lines of Yogi Bear or Huckleberry Hound, make eyes and mouth holes, and attach a section of an endless roll of elastic she had saved in the "rolls of things that defied description" drawer. Then, after positioning the mask on my face, I would sneak into the back room and make an ominous sound, to which my grandfather would first show great fear and then great joy at my arrival.

It was my grandfather who saved my life one day. On that day, he taught me to look both ways before I cross the road. It seems like it would be an easy lesson, but obviously I had not understood, or perhaps in my youthful enthusiasm to inspire my grandfather, I forgot that the blind curve of Roxbury Road in front of our house was a very dangerous place.

On my way for a visit, Corn Flakes box in hand, a car—or a truck? Memory does not serve—came to a screeching halt within feet of me. My grandfather picked me up, said something cordial but stern to the driver, carried me toward his porch, and scolded me all the way. I'm sure I was scared and crying, but I do not remember. I'm also sure that he was angry and scared himself, but I know he did not punish me.

He sat me down.

"Don't ever do that again," he said, calmly.

I can assure you, I never have.

My grandfather passed when I was four. While I can remember the days of running back into the shop and making a noise to get his attention, I have no visual image of him, only the sense of comfort that I had when he held me and the strong sound of his voice when he spoke.

My own father was a strict disciplinarian. He worked hard and expected his sons, who worked with him, to put in a good day's work. As soon as I could walk, I would accompany him on treks to the farmyard to feed the animals, milk cows, collect eggs, watch, and learn. There was so much equipment in our farmyard that there was almost never a day growing up when everything worked when it needed to. There was always so much to do that if you started a job and something broke, you could drop that job, start something else, and do it again several times before you had to go back to the original task and start all over again. This was not one of my father's best traits. In fact, as I grew up, I realized it was quite frustrating for us to want to get a job done but face these insurmountable, mechanical failures—and then spend hours of wasted time to fix whatever it was that was broken. I find myself even today struggling with this fractured gene in my DNA.

I have often said that I come from a long line of grass cutters. That is because most of the men who grew up in rural Vermont and owned large patches of land had to cut grass and process hay to feed the animals they kept on their farm. I grew up in that culture. Years later, I would come back to it when my father, having realized that animal farming was not a profitable business for him later in life, ventured into a career he called "custom farming," which would require him to work several hours daily to kludge some piece of the vast empire of equipment together so he could do whatever thirty-minute job was at hand for a reasonable hourly rate with his Massey Ferguson tractor.

I should probably state modestly at this point that at nine years old, I was an expert tractor driver. At thirty-five, I was so courageous that I felt I could drive a tractor up the side of any building and down again. My father instilled that confidence. While these machines were not the massive tractors of the Midwest, they had incredible power and a wide wheelbase that could turn challenging terrain to flat landscape.

Most of my memories of my father involve riding with him on the route, delivering milk for the local dairy or eggs to local homes, riding in the back of the bus as he drove hundreds of school children to and from school each day, or ushering at church twice a year, laughing hysterically at Ken Curtis as Festus Haggen on *Gunsmoke* every Monday night, and driving a tractor in a hayfield.

The difference in the ages of my brothers and my older sister would eventually leave me alone in the house with my parents when I was twelve. It was perhaps the busiest time in my father's professional life, as he worked a full-time job at Norwich, the local university, in the transportation and maintenance area during the school year, devoted summers to farmwork, and maintained a small empire of chickens and assorted other low-maintenance farm animals. Without the support of the older boys, all the work would fall to him or to me. I admit that at twelve, I was not responsible at all. For my father, the writing was on the wall.

I recall very clearly him asking me one day if I ever wanted to follow in his footsteps: ever wanted to take over the farm, sell the eggs, cut the grass, and perhaps expand the farm back to the twenty to thirty head of Guernsey milk cows we had years before.

"There are major repairs and upgrades to be made on the farm," he said. "We would need to open up new tracts of land or property, and all of it could be quite a good life."

I hesitated for a moment.

I looked at him and told him that I thought I would not want to work as hard as he had worked in his life. I felt that farming in Vermont, while an excellent life, might not be enough for me—that I would want to get out and see more of the world, and understand how other people live.

That day, my father decided to give up farming. He was perhaps forty-six or forty-seven. Over the course of the next three years, we gradually reduced our livestock business, and he moved permanently into his "custom farming" model—something he would always enjoy: driving a tractor into an enormous field of soon-to-be-cut grass and driving away two hours later with all of the fodder in neat, symmetrical rows awaiting the next implement in the process. For a decade or more, he had corner on the market in our hometown—a master tractor operator who could do any job.

It is said that you have to make hay when the sun shines. Despite the weather that prevails in the Northeast in the summer, it seemed like there were fewer and fewer sunny days and more and more of every other kind of day. Hay-producing farmers like my father had to be perceptive schedulers and weathermen, and extremely agile to react at any moment, and, once the time came, work nonstop to get the job done.

Cutting the grass was only the first step in the process. Depending on the time of day and temperature, it could be too humid for the grass to dry. We used a hay-tedding machine to allow air in and around the grass to help the process forward. The tedding almost always had to be done twice early in the haying season because of the rich thickness of the grass. Then we would roll the massive matt of curing grass into neat, bushy rows perfectly sized to be scooped up by the hay-baler rolling across the field in third gear, low range.

As I grew up, I would take part in the tedding, raking, and trucking part of the operation because there were fewer potential risks if I made a mistake in this process. In retrospect, cutting grass with a side mower or a mower conditioner presented enormous challenges, from avoiding branches and logs from river overflow to watching out for live animals nestled in the waist-high grass. Years later, I would understand those challenges, but at the time, I argued with my father to allow me to do it all. In the end, it was clear that our old equipment required his experienced touch.

My father always tried to make me a stronger and better worker. I was a typical product of the early '60s. At nearly nine years old, I grieved over the Kennedy assassination. I can still feel the odd change in the rhythm of daily life that great tragedy brought upon our country. As a young boy, I was confused that anyone could be so ruthless as to take the life of another person. As the Vietnam War escalated, and my older brother went off to serve in Germany, the mood on our farm changed.

Like his father before him, my father would save my life one day.

In my early teens, I did not have to argue with my father to take on more responsibility, particularly when it involved driving anything. On one occasion, he asked me to go with him to the top of Winch Hill where he had just completed a job. He told me to get on the tractor and drive it back home on the main road, which was about two miles away. It is a steep and curving hill to the main road, and although he said to leave the tractor in any low range and ride it slowly down the hill, it just did not seem to be going fast enough for me. So I took it out of gear, placed it in neutral, and when it was going faster than it should be going, I decided to simply turn off the engine altogether.

Now I quietly cruised down the hill like a bat out of hell.

As I made the last turn before I would crash over a ledge, I could see my father standing outside his truck, jumping up and down yelling to me, "Get on the brakes! Get on the brakes!"

I was large for my age, but not strong. So I stood up on the tractor and, with all my might, pushed down the left and right brakes with my right foot until I could not press any farther. The rear wheels locked and created a one-foot divot for ten feet in the road—and massive divots in the rich topsoil leading up to the ledge. The tractor came to a jarring stop. I immediately jumped off and began to head for home on foot, shaking and scared. I was sure I would never drive a tractor again.

A father could have done all sorts of things at that moment. Dad was certainly angry, and I cannot remember the exact words he said, but I do remember him grabbing me by the back of my collar and flinging me back around in the direction of the tractor.

"Come on, boy," he said. "Get back up on that thing and drive it home."

If I argued, and I am sure I did, it would not have made a difference. I got back on the tractor and drove the last quarter mile home to our farm with my father following me—at a top speed of about two miles an hour!

There is a small sense of fearlessness in operating heavy machinery. I've known many experienced people who have, in an instant, lost their lives performing relatively simple tasks. I've also witnessed less-experienced operators crashing on small jobs around their homes with equipment that was extremely hazardous or used in unsafe conditions. In our small community, we would mourn the casualties of these accidents, and speak well of the people who were no longer with us, and then my father would be sure to discuss it with me so I could learn from their mistakes. That is how my father became such an excellent tractor operator—and an excellent people operator, too.

Years later, I received a call one day that my father had been having some fainting spells in the field. The spells had been going on for a couple of weeks, but he had alerted no one. My mother discovered what was happening and forced him into the doctor's office. The doctor determined that a pacemaker would be in order. All this was fine. It was Friday. The operation would occur the following Monday.

The problem was that it was early spring, and that weekend would be the biggest garden rototilling days of the season. My father, in his rather stubborn way, wanted to continue to work through the weekend to complete the most lucrative part of his "custom farming" business.

So it was with some surprise that he greeted me when I showed up at five on Saturday morning from New York City for breakfast with him at home. When he asked why I was there, I said that I was ready to go to work on the tractor for the next couple days. I was perhaps twenty-six years old and had not driven a tractor for at least nine years, but I convinced him it would be just like riding a bike. He argued back that I'd never successfully rototilled a garden, that there was a lot involved, and that he didn't have time to show me what I needed to know, so I should just stay home and drink coffee with my mother. He did not consider the possibility that I had learned something from him through the years. He relented and off we went.

In the first two gardens, I received a crash course from my father on how to effectively rototill a garden—and leave the plot without a tractor-tire track, which was his professional signature of a job well done. I will not share the involved technique here because there might be a time in my future when I'll need that skill again. I distinctly remember that my father was an excellent teacher, that I learned quickly, and that the years of driving a tractor as a boy and young man would always be part of my skill set as a human being.

Halfway through the third garden, my father collapsed in the field watching me. At that moment, he realized he was mortal, agreed that we both had had enough of this, and we canceled the rest of the activities for the weekend. I sat with him through Sunday afternoon until it started to rain and I was sure that he could not venture back out until after his surgery the following morning.

Over the next several years, I took an increased interest in the "custom farming" business, using the sidebar mower and bush hog more often and venturing out to pasture alone—driving a tractor through all kinds of different situations—when I visited town each summer on vacation.

It was not until my father was diagnosed with acute leukemia at sixty-seven years old that I realized I wanted to live closer to my parents and settle down with my family in my hometown. I started making plans to move from New York City back to Vermont. No one could predict that in the months that followed our move in 1989, my mother would die in advance of my father.

In the last months with his disease, my father's courage and strength of will is something I will never forget. From his hospital bed, we talked about rototilling gardens, his complex little-black-book record-keeping system for garden locations of virtually everyone in town, and the mysteries of a forty-year-old hay baler—the only implement that I had never operated. He solved that mystery and gave me some outstanding advice for virtually any project I'd take on in the future. His final words on the topic still ring in my head:

"Don't make the row too wide," he told me. "You need to be able to keep a consistent ground speed to get the job done on time, so the rows must be consistent to keep the machine from jamming up. And it's all in your preparation. The hay has to be cut and dried properly, shaped into even rows, and then it's just a matter of driving along until the job is done."

Father's Day is one of those special days each year. Our fathers teach us so many wonderful things that we take for granted, that it is hard to sort one from the other, until the years have passed, and we reflect on what happened along the way. I love and respect all those I have come to think are just like a father to me. But the fact is, on Father's Day, my thoughts go back to the man himself.

Happy Father's Day.

JUNE 20, 2009

CHAPTER 26

MY DEAR EDWARD

My dear Edward,

Thank you so much for sharing with me your reflections on your dad. What a special guy!

Having not grown up on a farm, I really enjoyed the detailed picture of what life on the farm is really like—no picnic, to say the least. And yet it is clear that your many wonderful personal traits are as a result of that special, tough, memorable upbringing. I only wish your dad were here to read your remarkable essay. Did I ever tell you what a good writer you are? You are a master of detail, which is the stuff of the best writing. Again, thanks for sharing that with me and Happy, Happy Father's Day, dear sir!

John C.

PS I hasten to add that I am so glad you survived the runaway tractor incident and that you lived to tell this story!

JUNE 21, 2009

My last email from John Callaway

Act I, Scene 6

I have cognitive dysfunction
Some call it "Chemo Brain."
It's just a symptom of the cure they say
That will help my cancer go away to stay.

Impatient Patient
Act I Scene 6

CHAPTER 27

ACT I, SCENE 6

SETTING: TRANSITION: Blue Room to
            Administrator's Office

SONGS: CHEMO BRAIN
            TOO MUCH INFORMATION
            BIG BUSINESS

AT RISE: The IMPATIENT PATIENT and the ORDERLY
            roll center from the Blue Room scene
            and sing CHEMO BRAIN.

Lights dim as scene changes to the Administrator's
Office. The CHIEF presents to members of the board.
He is nervous and the mood is grim.

JOE GORILLA is among them in disguise. The CHAOSALS
stand by in disguise, one on top of the other's
shoulders. Large trend graphs show red indicators
heading down while black indicators are flat.

CHIEF sings TOO MUCH INFORMATION and concludes that
the treatment center will either have to develop
a more aggressive long-range expansion plan, or

go with his recommendation that all treatment
facilities close and patient care transfers to the
new regional facility north of the city.

THOMPSON enters as the CHIEF concludes. He apologizes
to the board for being late but has overheard
enough to take an immediate and passionate stand
for continuation of care at the center. The CHIEF
tells him that it's all business: "Big Business!"
He sings BIG BUSINESS with the rest the board and
JOE joining in.

THOMPSON watches helplessly as the board shows
overwhelming support for the CHIEF's plan to move
forward with a feasibility study to close the
center, headed by JOE as the consultant.

As JOE steps forward to present the feasibility
plan, he pitches an absurd advertising and marketing
campaign concept to the board to raise awareness
and sponsorship for the future, as well as to
boost the image of the center and the move. With
the CHIEF as spokesman and the board enthusiastic,
everyone feels good, except for THOMPSON, who is
doubtful and despondent.

All exit, leaving THOMPSON alone and troubled.

CHEMO BRAIN

RULE NO. 5: APOLOGIZE in advance for chemo brain fog.

Noticing your shortfalls during this treatment keeps those around you in touch with your feelings. I have never been as irritable as I am now. I know it comes from either the frustration of dealing with this disease day after day, or perhaps from the realization that just as I start to feel a little better, I have to go back and do it again.

In between, I struggle to continue a somewhat normal but vastly reduced work schedule, plan a wedding and a move, and almost daily wrestle with this odd fog in my head that makes me lose something of value each day. I find it eventually, so no real harm is done, but after a while, how many times can you look for your keys or your cell phone without getting irritated?

So I take a deep breath and think about it all logically. The fog clears for a moment, and I find whatever it is. Last night it was one glove: I found it in an unlikely place, only to realize that I had found the other glove—the one that wasn't missing. Very nearly threw out the first glove this morning because I was convinced the mate had fallen in the street.

One of the best things about finding something you thought you lost is the joyous feeling of discovering you still have it. After I figured that out, I began to make a fun little game of looking for whatever it is.

Then, the irritation passes and I get on with the day. Once in a while, Denise plays my little game with me, and we earnestly search high and low for whatever I think I lost only to find it right where it was all along.

In truth, I lost Denise a couple times. I am thankful that she allowed me to find her again.

Which brings me to Rule No. 6: Accept that those closest to you feel everything you do.

CHAPTER 29

PEOPLE I KNEW—
JASON SEGAL, NU '60

Dear Mary Jo,

I want you to know that I have started and stopped writing this letter several times over the past two months until I finally realized that no matter how much I wanted to say, the words were not coming out right. Denise and I were shaken by the news of Jason's situation, and his passing was so very sad for us. I am sorry that I could not have been more in the present with you, and I hope that, in some small way, this letter will let you know how Jason, and everything he did, made a difference in my life. With the time to reflect on so many things, I wanted to write something personal.

It is hard for me to believe that I am in my sixtieth year. I was a young man, eager and fearless, when I returned to Northfield to work at Norwich in 1989. Jason and Bob were already old then, I thought—probably fifty-one or so.

What I wouldn't give to be fifty years old now!

It was my choice to leave New York City and a promising career to come home. I decided it was more important to face my father's mortality head-on than from a distance. I became an active player in his support system, trying to help my mother and sister, who had been carrying the full weight of his illness. There was also the opportunity to give my nine-year-old daughter a better life and a closer bond with her grandparents and cousins. And then, perhaps, a change of scenery might breathe new life into my marriage, which it did, for a time.

I wanted to move back home because it was a place I could believe in, with people around me I cared about. That passion showed in my early development work and was magnified three-fold after Norwich stood by me when both of my parents passed in the first year. That year, I met Jason, Bob, Barry Meinerth, Carlo D'Este, Ron Lotz, Bob Mack, John Swift, Yank Shugg, and many others who became fast friends, mentors, and older brothers.

Perhaps you and Pep know better than anyone how important Jason and Bob were to me at that time in my life. Their support, encouragement and care for me was remarkable. Thinking back on it now, I'm convinced that they were tag-teaming me, making sure that I wouldn't fly off the handle, implode, and disappear in a puff of smoke.

Despite all their efforts, I did step aside as the politics swirled and Norwich wrestled with leadership challenges—issues I clearly accept now at sixty but had little understanding about then. My forty-year-old self would never return to the same level of enthusiasm and zeal at Norwich that I once had. I was much more skeptical and found that my trust level was shaken. But at both Jason and Bob's urging, I took a deep breath, considered the options, and, over the last few years at Norwich, stabilized my life and got back on board to do the work that was expected of me.

Had they not intervened, I do not know where I would be today.

In all the years that I was at Norwich, and for a decade after when we continued to produce the Colby and helped support the Sullivan Museum and Wise Center from Chicago, I never lost my respect for Norwich's leadership, her goals, or mission, as well as the wonderful alumni and extraordinary students. I also never drifted too far away from Jason and Bob, who always stayed in touch, offering the same unconditional support and encouragement they always did. I only wish I could have given back more of the same to both of them along the way.

My move to Chicago was a fresh start, at the beginning of a project filled with expectation, promise, and excitement. I made a pact with myself that I would not be single-minded in my approach to this opportunity, choosing consciously to stop and smell the roses once in a while. A hopeless workaholic, I soon realized that life's rhythm again consumed me. It was all wildly exciting. Over time, the feelings of remorse and regret I had at leaving my life behind in Vermont was filled with the success of the library and the opportunity to live and work in Chicago. I would literally run to work a block away and privately hoped they never discovered that I would probably do the job for nothing. That enthusiasm became infectious to the team working on the project. We all realized we were doing something important, meaningful, and permanent.

Curiously, that's the same feeling I had at Norwich in those early days almost twenty-five years ago.

In the first several years in Chicago, Norwich hockey was very important. I listened to the internet broadcast as a lifeline to my hometown. I was still producing the Colby, responding to lots of personal and foundation queries, and managing how we might continue to remain involved with a host of other priorities. I now served on another staff and under restricted guidelines. Unpopular decisions were never mine to make, but I was always the messenger. As responsibilities grew here, my connections to Vermont and my Norwich allies became more distant. Life's rhythm had shifted, but Jason and Bob were always there.

Six years ago June, I was diagnosed with stage 3C colon cancer. Nothing would be the same.

Late that summer, after my surgery and during chemotherapy, I contacted Jason and worked with him to design Denise's engagement ring. He had always told me if I ever needed some help, to let him know. I think I may have gotten some other items, but this was big—important—and I didn't have a clue!

Jason was calm about the whole thing. All I'd need was Denise's ring size and he'd take care of the rest, I seem to recall him saying. That ring-size thing would prove to be the challenge.

You need to know, at this point, that Denise is a big fan of the film *Moonstruck* and had said often, "When you propose to a woman, you gotta have a ring," so I was not going to make that mistake. Still, I could not think of a creative way to get her ring size, as she was involved in the planning of a huge event at the time, insanely busy, and very distracted. I could not ask her mother for help. I could guess, but Jason said that was a bad idea. We talked a lot about this at the time. I consulted some friends. One said to bring a new bowling ball home for sizing. That was one of the better ideas, actually.

So, one night while she was changing in the bedroom after a particularly rough day, I decided to just take the plunge, which I now attribute to a bad decision by a guy on chemotherapy. I walked up to her and said quietly, "I need to ask you a question in a few weeks, but before I can, I need to know your ring size." Her eyes started to well up, and she said, "Are you asking me to marry you?" "No," I said. "I am asking you for your ring size. It would not be right to propose to a woman without a ring." Denise started immediately to hyperventilate, crying out, "You chose the busiest weekend of my life to come in here when I am half naked and ask me for my ring size, but you are NOT asking me to marry you?!"

"That's about right," I said.

You know the rest. She calmed down and we got the information. Jason had the most beautiful ring I have ever seen made for Denise. In a couple of weeks, we had dinner in the antique elevator booth of Hugo's Frog Bar, where I asked her to marry me and slipped the ring on her finger—a perfect fit. It glistened in the dim light of the booth, and all the way home it was a beacon of color and light.

Our ring, Jason's kindness, and your friendship will always bring color and light to our lives. We have a small reminder of his generous spirit, and my life is so much more enriched by having you and Jason as a part of so many wonderful adventures.

That restless young man who lived a charmed life in Vermont for so many years is a little more hardened and pragmatic these days—the culmination of all the experiences and the people who have walked along the path with me and often carried me along through difficult times.

Jason and I talked late last summer. I had realized one day that I had not heard from him in a while and picked up the phone to call. I recall that he told me that some tests would be taken, that the company had given him a pension position of some sort that he was very proud of, and that he may have implied that something more serious was going on, but the tone of the conversation did not give me a sense at all of how serious things might be.

I think that's the way he may have wanted it.

Mary Jo, please know that I think of you often, hope you are well, and pray that our warm thoughts reach you and wrap you with comfort and love.

FEBRUARY 24, 2014

CHAPTER 30

THE VOICE OF NORWICH HOCKEY

ON ANY GIVEN Friday and Saturday in my first full year in Chicago, I would plan to work late and listen to the online broadcast of Norwich hockey with play-by-play by George Commo.

That broadcast—which originated as Mike McShane arrived as head coach and the university was building the most advanced new arena in Division III hockey, Kreitzberg Arena—resulted from an arrangement negotiated with radio station WDEV's owner, Ken Squier. Commo and his broadcast partner, Dave Moody, who engineered announcements and provided color commentary, emerged as college hockey's top radio broadcast team.

The year Kreitzberg opened, Norwich dominated their division, was ranked first in the national D-III polls, and hosted the 1999 NCAA Division III Men's Ice Hockey Tournament in Northfield. But the team fell short of capturing the national championship, losing the semi-final to Wisconsin-Superior and then watching the Middlebury College Panthers disassemble the Yellowjackets to win their fifth national title in a row.

And although the big prize did not come to Northfield to stay in Coach McShane's fourth year at Norwich, the Cadets won over

Vermont fans through the live broadcast of Norwich hockey on WDEV with Commo, Moody, and me serving as statistician and wingman.

Redoubling efforts, and with an ever-expanding fan network, the Norwich Cadets responded with an undefeated season in league play (with one tie) the following year and another memorable run through the postseason on their way to the Frozen Four and a return match in the semi-final with the Wisconsin-Superior Yellowjackets, this time at Wessman Arena in Superior, Wisconsin.

Hundreds of Norwich fans—dubbed "the Kreitzberg Krazies" by Commo and Moody—made the trek west to see Norwich top the Yellowjackets in a Saint Patrick's Day thriller, 5–4, and then return a day later to earn a hard-fought 2–1 victory over the St. Thomas Tommies to win the first-ever NCAA Men's Hockey National Championship in Norwich history. We were on the road and in the booth for every game that championship season, a sign of great things to come for the program and a partnership that led to expanding the broadcast to other media platforms.

Except for news highlights, it would be days later before Vermont fans actually saw the stunning defeat of Wisconsin-Superior, when Casey Beaulac scored to seal the victory and sent the Cadets into the championship.

But the Green Mountains shook that night from Brattleboro to Burlington.

"Goodbye, Superior!" was the call by Commo.

The most memorable call ever.

As technology advanced, the broadcast emerged on video, and quickly the Norwich Cadets, one of the top teams in the nation, was being broadcast on television across the state.

More than twenty years and three more national championships later, George Commo called the play-by-play for arguably one of the best teams in Norwich history during the 2019–2020 season with an overall 24–2–2 record. The Cadets were undefeated in their last eighteen games (including two ties), the last nine shutouts by Tom

Aubrun, who has since signed with the Rockford Ice Hogs of the American Hockey League, an affiliate of the Chicago Blackhawks—and were preparing to host the quarterfinal round of the NCAA D-III championships when the COVID-19 pandemic shuttered the school and, with it, all intercollegiate sports.

However things might have turned out, one thing is known for sure: Norwich Hall-of-Famer George Commo, the longtime "Voice of Norwich Hockey," would have been there making the call.

MARCH 17, 2020

CHAPTER 31

GEORGE COMMO—
PLAY-BY-PLAY

(A Monologue)

IMAGINE BEING PERCHED ON the back of a creaky wooden chair, high above the fray . . .

You plant your feet firmly in such a way that you can rise up at any moment over the fans in front of you to catch the action.

Side to side.

Back and forth.

For the better part of three hours.

Talking all the time. Lecturing briskly. To a very good friend. Or perhaps several hundred very good friends all gathered around you in a room. Or a thousand miles away. Or perhaps next door. Or across the arena.

You tell them what you see. Bring it to life as you absorb yourself in the game. Pause only occasionally to peer at notes strewn across a narrow table. Pen in hand. Stats cross every which way. Fill the dead air with just enough enthusiasm to carry to the next moment.

And when there's a "time-out," you're "ON"! In fact, you're always "ON" as long as there's power to the remote and a good engineer back at the studio.

The game is your friend.

The players are the story.

All of them performing. Excelling. Their pride at stake. Smashing and crashing to victory. Bringing the crowd to its feet with a spectacular effort. A sequence your friends know intensifies by the elevated excitement in your voice. A tone they have heard before. Dozens of times. Screaming above the chaos of the crowd and groundswell of emotion. A frenzy of sounds and dialogue. Culminating in a tumultuous roar.

And then, your silence.

When all your friends know that, for a moment, they are by your side. Having seen exactly what you have told them you saw. Feeling that moment like it was there in front of them. Exactly at that moment. Hundreds of miles away. Or next door. Waiting for the next word. The next time. The next groundswell of emotion.

Opening a door in your imagination is just one part of great play-by-play broadcasting. Whether it is winning a national championship or a hard-fought high school basketball game, the game's the thing. To tell the story, you must paint a thousand pictures. You are artist, historian, statistician, psychologist, author, broadcaster, coach, critic, and above all, the consummate communicator who recalls in words what has happened in an instant. A truly remarkable gift!

It's always been the thrill of a lifetime or a bittersweet lesson. Each one a part of *your* great game!

Thanks and congratulations, George!

You're the best!

George Commo Day at Norwich University

AUGUST 20, 2003

CHAPTER 32

DEAR JOHN—LEGACIES

Dear John,

I have been thinking a lot recently about legacies.

Our existence is built on the legacies of those who have come before us—their ideals, values, and the lessons we have been taught without understanding that we were even in school at the time. It feels like an obligation to pass these experiences from one generation to the next so that we never forget how we got where we are and what we have learned.

I have felt that the essence of who we become in life is a result of every human interaction and experience we have. The memories of experiences we are witness to in our families are every bit as important as anything tangible that may be left behind.

Those experiences are then transferred to our living legacies: those we give life to, nurture, and protect, and spend most of our waking moments hoping will prosper and achieve their full potential. I am sure that you and I could spend some time discussing our own shortcomings. But I prefer to recall moments so illuminating that they capture my imagination and interest in drilling down to relive them all over again.

That exercise seems like a much better investment of my time.

Long ago, there was a country minister who served in World War II and settled down to a quiet life and a small church in Roxbury, Vermont. He was a remarkable writer and orator, and those who knew John Evans looked to him for guidance, comfort, and friendship at some of the most conflicted times of their lives. He worked every day to make the world a better place for those he came in touch with through sixty-five years in the ministry. He brought a different point of view to the fellowship of those he knew, trying to understand what was necessary for each person individually while communicating a message that could be heard by everyone who passed his way.

John was a sincere and genuinely present human being.

Roxbury is still, perhaps, one of the smallest villages in the country with a resident population of about 500. There are several small businesses, a free library, bed and breakfast, a summer camp, and community potluck dinners two times a month. There is also a small church in the center of Roxbury which was home to John Evans's ministry for many years.

Following the passing of my mother and for several years after, John and I would share special times at Norwich University's homecoming each year, recalling those who had passed on the year before. It seems that death always brought John and me closer together. I enjoyed the time we spent, and we often said that we should get together for dinner or a visit. I do not recall any of those opportunities actually occurring, but I always heard from John Evans when he knew our family needed him most. Often that was in the form of a note, a letter or a phone call. It was always personal and respectful, but more importantly, truthful and comforting. He knew just what to say and how to say it.

My mother passed away quite suddenly a few days after her sixty-sixth birthday in 1989. My father, fighting a battle for his life with acute leukemia, sat up stunned and silent in his recliner in the living room of the house my parents had built on our farm. John Evans sat next to him on the couch, engaging my father in a conversation about his health and treatments. The house was hot from the wood fire in the furnace, the kind of fire that often required us to open the door for fresh air.

It was on this day that my father ventured into the only discussion I recall him engaging in about religion. It was my mother's influence that brought us to the Methodist church school, summer camp, and Sunday services. Ever the good citizen, my father ushered two Sundays a year in church and participated in christenings, weddings, funerals, and other community events, but I do not recall ever seeing my father holding a Bible or asking us to join in prayer, although he participated when called upon to do so.

Early in the conversation, my father had asked John to conduct the service and deliver the eulogy for my mother. Then I was surprised when my father leaned forward in his chair and started talking less about the funeral arrangements and more about church and the ministry.

"John," he said, "you know that I have never been a religious man. I am not sure what I should be doing."

Pausing for a moment, John Evans said quietly, "Wayne, it's natural to be confused at a time like this, but there is one thing you can be sure of: You may not think you are a religious man, but there's no doubt that you have lived your life religiously. It's our spirituality—who we are and the faith that it is built on— and how we apply those values, not where we pray or how often we join together as a group," he said.

"You are a remarkable man, Wayne," he continued. "You have been devoted to your community, a hard worker, a good husband, and a good father to your wonderful family. You have led a full, decent, and respectful life. And you have influenced more people than you will ever know."

Then, John Evans looked straight at my father and said, "Even though you don't realize it, you have given unconditional love and comfort to many, particularly to Helen, when she needed it most. Whether or not you pray publicly or privately, the message is heard."

John Evans put my father's mind at ease that day. The subject never came up again.

I came across a copy of John's eulogy not long ago—a wonderful piece of writing recalling my mother speeding across the wide expanse of our lower field alone on her snowmobile in the winter, toiling in the garden on a hot summer day, or sitting outside on the lawn watching the neighbors go by. John had included, with the printed copy of his homily, a personal letter telling me how sorry he was that she had passed, that our two families had a special connection, and that he hoped that I would call on him for anything in the future.

My father passed away five months later, and John Evans was there for our family. This time, though, John talked about my father's living legacy, my brothers and sister, and the good work we have all done, as well as the essence of the person who emerges within us. I didn't think much about it at the time, but over the years, those words became important to me.

John and Mary Evans left living legacies of their own. One of them is their son, Peter.

Growing up in a small town in Vermont was not without its challenges. The guys in school all called each other by our father's names, or by their occupation, in those days. So, on any day I could be "Wayne" or "the Eggman." There was "Cheesy," and "Fel," "Dallas," "Guy," and "Roland." Peter was "John" or "Rev," as I recall, but he might correct me on that today. I clearly remember him calling me "Wayne" for most of my young-adult life. Peter was a year older and married his high school sweetheart, Debbie. We all went to UVM but, as friends do, drifted apart for a decade or more after high school.

When I came back to town, Peter was teaching at Northfield High School, and we quickly were reacquainted through the evolving drama program, working together on projects—including one in particular for *Annie Get Your Gun*, which featured my daughter, Amanda, as Annie. Peter headed the industrial arts program, but he was much more than that to the school and the community. He committed his energy to Northfield with the same kind of spirit and enthusiasm as our fathers. He was a great colleague, teacher, and friend.

A few years later, Peter moved on to be principal at Montpelier High School, and after a superb career, he recently retired to pursue projects that interest him, including pottery and a portable wood-milling operation, complete with a Massey Ferguson tractor, my father's workhorse of choice.

Peter, like our fathers before us, has blended into the rich fabric of a sleepy town in Vermont where wonderful people are doing good things to make the world a better place.

I have always considered myself a spiritual person, but living a religious life was not something I did consciously. As my father inched toward the end of his life, my sister and I spent more time with him in and out of the hospital. My nephew, Nate, an Air Force veteran, had moved in to help on a day-to-day basis. Friends stopped by regularly for short visits.

They were saying goodbye.

In early May, five months after my mother had passed, I booked an overnight train with my first wife, Mary, to New York City. The plan was to stay in New York for a few days while I worked for the university. We had not been away together alone in many months.

It was Mother's Day, and the family had gathered for a memorial service and interment at Hope Cemetery. When it came time, Dad did not feel well enough to attend. After lunch, as we prepared to leave for the train station, my sister called and said that Dad was headed back into the hospital in the afternoon.

When I stopped by to see him, I had already started making travel changes. He told me that he was going back in because he felt that they could make him feel more comfortable after the recent chemotherapy treatment and that we should go to New York. It wasn't really a request, as I recall.

"Are you going to be here when I get back?" I asked.

"One way or the other," he said.

We left on the overnight Amtrak train that departs from Montpelier and weaves its way through the Green Mountains through Northfield and past the homestead at about 9:30 every night. We checked in early the next morning in a hotel, showered, and had a busy, productive day in the city.

That night, I called and spoke with my father in the hospital. He had been evaluated and was comfortable, but the doctors had told him there was not a lot they could do at this point. My sister went into the details a little later. The doctors had advised that we should be prepared for a lengthy situation: weeks or perhaps months.

After a restless night and some meetings on Tuesday, I went to St. Patrick's Cathedral late in the afternoon and prayed for my father. I can recall all of it exactly in my mind, even as I write: where I was in the church, how quiet everything was, and how peaceful I felt when I left.

That evening, after dinner, we returned to the hotel room and discovered a message from my sister to call. My father had passed away a few hours before—soon after I left the cathedral.

We returned home and my father's services followed. My parents had passed exactly five months apart. I questioned how hard they'd had to work to provide for their family, thought about their individual contributions to the community, and mourned how much their grandchildren would miss their presence growing up and becoming parents themselves.

Far off in the distance one night as I sat on the deck of the log cabin, I could hear the approaching Amtrak train. My thoughts raced back to the week before, being on that train, away from my father, and the sadness of the realization that it had been the last day I had seen him alive. As the train came closer, it had a fearful, haunting sound. I realized that every night going forward, the train would pass, and with it would come the reminder of that day and that I was not with him.

No one told me at the time that the feeling was natural or that it would change in time, that I had done all that any man could have done to be a good son to his father. I had left a promising position in New York to return home to Northfield to help my family cope. It took a long time to process all that happened in those months and to recognize that there are sights, sounds, and smells that trigger our memories of those closest to us in a powerful way.

For weeks after this first revelation, I heard the approaching train go by at the same time each day. Some nights, my daughter, Amanda, and I would plan on it—a time to spend together at sunset. In time, I referred to it as Dad's Train.

And over the years, and to this day, the sound of a train whistle reminds me of him as a comforting and welcome sound. It has rippled through a silent moment at family weddings or other significant events as if he is letting me know he's watching, listening, and proud of all of us.

Last night, I sat in Viper Alley while your living legacies—Liz Callaway and Ann Hampton Callaway—performed their cabaret show *Boom*. It included music of the '60s, and they related memories of their own growing-up—the maple bedroom set that Ann had in her room and a spirited performance of my sister's favorite Petula Clark song.

After the concert, Ann and Liz told me that it felt like family was here and that your presence was in the room, warming the place, and that they felt the magnificent expression of pride and love you had when you watched your girls do the things you loved seeing them do.

It's nice to know that we can still count on the little things to bring us joy, whether it is a letter from a good friend or a warm thought of days gone by.

I have felt that the essence of who we become in life is a result of every human interaction and experience we have. The memories of experiences we are witness to in our families are every bit as important as anything tangible that may be left behind.

Those experiences are then transferred to our living legacies: those we give life to, nurture, and protect, and spend most of our waking moments hoping will prosper and achieve their full potential.

I am sure that you and I could spend some time discussing our own shortcomings. But I prefer to recall moments so illuminating that they capture my imagination and interest in drilling down to relive them all over again.

That exercise seems like a much better investment of my time.

I hope you enjoyed the show, my friend.

JUNE 2, 2020

Act I, Scene 7

There's a fantasy I think about
when things are dark and gray.
It's a journey to a blissful place
A land not far away.
I know I've never been there and
it seems so quaintly real
To spend a day away from all this sorrow
and think what I'd do
with a tomorrow.

Tess Terone
Act I, Scene 7

CHAPTER 33

ACT I, SCENE 7

SETTING: Chemotherapy Treatment Room

SONG: THIS IS WHAT I'D DO WITH A TOMORROW

AT RISE: At dusk, the staff prepares to close the
             treatment room. Patients and caregivers
             gather their belongings.

TESS sings THIS IS WHAT I'D DO WITH A TOMORROW.
The stage evolves from the treatment center to an
imaginary exterior scene of bright colors as each
of the principal's aspirations are realized in a
dream sequence.

As the COMPANY number concludes, the set reverts to
the treatment center exterior and the ENSEMBLE exit.

THOMPSON and CHIEF can be seen through a building
window, involved in a heated discussion in the
examination room. JOE and the CHAOSALS appear in
another window, looking on.

                    FADE TO BLACK

                    END ACT I

CHAPTER 34

COLON CANCER IS A PREVENTABLE DISEASE

THOSE OF US IN "the Club" know how important the support network is—the calls, cards, and other expressions that come from those close friends who mean more than anyone knows.

I have taken the position that people I meet need to know I am undergoing chemotherapy.

I tell them the most important thing to me is that they understand the importance of a colonoscopy.

Twenty of my closest friends have confided that they have gotten the exam since hearing about my condition. It is particularly important to have the test if you have had cancer in your family. It is vitally important if there is a history of colon cancer. In this regard, I always say, forty is the new fifty. Early detection is key.

Colonoscopies—what you remember of them—aren't fun, but they're not as horrifying as you might think. You fast for twenty-four hours; you drink a nasty-but-bearable substance; you spend some time getting rid of that substance; and then, the next day, you go in for an exam that, while they usually don't put you under, you don't remember because it's like the 1960s all over again: You're medicated to the point that you're not aware of the procedure as it's happening.

I am thankful each day that I have a supportive employer, caring friends, and a fabulous partner who have all helped me through this period.

I live physically close to the hospital, so getting in and out is easy. Living close by does not make the walk I am on less difficult, the challenge less daunting, or the unknown consequences less great. I understood that early on, and that is why I am grateful every day that there are well-meaning people beside me who care. It's important to me that I keep those loved ones for as long as I can.

Rule No. 7: With early detection, colon cancer can be an avoidable disease.

CHAPTER 35

DRIVING THE BASELINE; DRIVING THE BUS

I HAD THIS INCREDIBLE image of my father today. He was driving his Ford milk truck, which had the option of sitting in a seat or standing up to drive—something I did as a very young driver. We were on the way to a high school basketball game. I was playing—or rather, sitting on the bench, since we were one of the best teams in the state and I was one of the worst players on the team.

But I was on the team.

And did I mention it was one of the best in the state?

Our bench players substituted for the starters as long as we kept from losing the game after the starters had built an insurmountable lead. I was an excellent rebounder and passer, could dribble the ball, and was pretty smart on the court—but I was not much of a scorer. In fact, in three years and more than sixty games, I scored a total of fifty career points.

If you do the math, that's not impressive. Still, I lived for the cheerleaders to do their "Hoot! Hoot!" after we made a basket. Of course, the advantage is that not scoring many points makes practically every basket a vivid memory in your mind's eye—a moment when you are the only one between the basket and the ball going through it. And to hear the cheer that would rise up from all the cheerleaders when you did score . . .

My father was the president and one of the founding members of the Northfield Athletic Booster Club at Northfield High School. Years later, in the last years of his life, a small group of townspeople would recognize his contribution to the town of Northfield and to the athletic community. It was his association with the high school and Norwich University athletics that made him most proud.

For years he was the team bus driver. He loved driving anything, but particularly a bus. And when he wasn't driving, he was keeping official time for all home games. In his era, he was the official timekeeper for the school for boys' and girls' basketball and hockey, and then would keep score when he drove the bus for out-of-town games. He filled some of the same roles at Norwich. He loved sports.

He was proud of me for even making the team, but he knew secretly that, as much as I tried to be a better player, I did not have the size, skill, or technique of the other guys. I was better at piano and singing than swinging a bat. He once said—not in a bad way—that, just once, it would be great if I came out of my artistic shell and made the play of the game.

The NHS Booster Club would do anything to support Coach Zabek on the court. My dad facilitated the purchase of the school's first video camera so the team could record a game and watch it as part of their practice routine. Everyone was excited to see the scaffolding up high in the corner of the gym, with Ron Corliss, the student camera operator, on top taking it all in.

The game was unspectacular. Early in the first half, we were up by fifteen. The subs came in and maintained a ten-point lead at the half. Early in the second half, our two best players made stupid fouls and the coach pulled them out. When they tried to explain, Coach said, "It's all on video—we'll talk about it tomorrow."

So I had a chance to play that night. As I checked in at the scorekeeper table and onto the half-court line just in front of my dad, I caught his eye. He knew this was the chance I had been waiting for. I was sized well for this team and could move the ball if I wanted to. My dad didn't say a word. Looked at me and did not smile. He didn't have to.

My heart pumped wildly. I started to sweat—the kind of sweat that pours off your body and drips down your sides. I knew I'd have to get in and mix it up right away to establish some space under the basket—and to calm my nerves, or I would pass out from fear of failure.

On the first rotation, I passed off to the top of the key. On the shot, I cut into the basket and leaped for the rebound, which I got but, in the process, fouled the man in front of me. We were not in the penalty, so no shot resulted, but we lost possession of the ball.

Coming down the court, I heard Coach yell, "Aggressive play! Keep it up!" I crouched and taunted my man, trying to deny him the ball. He feinted out, then he tried to go backdoor on me, but I opened up on the cut and stole the ball, tossing quickly up court, turning up on a three-on-two at the other end.

I brought up the trailer, and, to my surprise, they passed the ball back out to me, rather than driving for the layup. The play broke to the left side and I cut right. From out in the far-right corner, I could see the rotation of the ball as it came back to me, with one man on me.

I faked into the basket, then cut back away to receive the pass. With ball in hand, I squared against my man, faked left, and he took it. The baseline was wide open. I dribbled hard to the basket, and, with my left hand, stuck a layup gently on the backboard from the right side and passed under the basket as it went in. The cheerleaders roared. I ran right past them and was sure that they smiled at me. It was that pretty a play.

Thanks to the power of videotape, we viewed my play over and over again on the tape the following day in practice. I would never get the baseline again but knew that, at least once, my father saw that I had the right stuff for the game.

Dad went home that night and told Mom in detail about the baseline drive I pulled off that night.

And he talked about it again over breakfast the following morning, just before he got back in his milk truck to go drive the bus.

CHAPTER 36

TV MOVIE TREATMENT—FORE

THERE ARE DAYS THAT you wake up and a murder mystery is on your mind.

This is one of those days:

It is spring. A garage door opens, and someone drags two barrels to the sidewalk. He tosses a spade into one of the barrels. He places a bag of golf clubs on the curb and closes the garage door. The trash hauler whisks the clubs off the curb, but rather than toss them in the back of the truck, he puts them in the cab. The trash hauler tosses the spade into a bin with other tools.

It is fall. An elderly woman inspects the golf clubs at a yard sale. She pays for them, and the seller puts the clubs in the back of the woman's car. She drives home.

In her kitchen, the woman prepares a small dinner, decorates a cake, and sets a table in her modest dining room. The woman's family arrives. After dinner, they all sing "Happy Birthday" to Dan, the woman's son. The golf clubs sit among the presents in the corner of the room.

The party winds down; the mother and son gather at his car. Dan places the clubs in the trunk of his car, alongside a flak jacket and detective gear.

It is morning. Dan enters city hall dressed in plain clothes with a weapon and detective badge.

A staff briefing includes discussion of overnight activity and daily assignments. As the meeting breaks, Dan talks with his colleagues about the weekend, the party, and the new "used" golf clubs—the continuation of a tradition his long-deceased father started. The group plans a golf outing.

On the putting green, Dan inspects the golf clubs for the first time. The bag is high end and the clubs are high quality. The set is incomplete: There is no driver or number five iron. The round continues. Drives. Putting. Chip shots. A great day on the course with friends.

The group leaves the club lounge. It is dusk. Dan puts the bag into the trunk of his car. He sees dark material caked on the bottom of the bag. Days pass and detective work continues. A case involving a shooting in a local neighborhood. A series of civil disputes.

Dan plays more golf. His game improves.

Dan visits a local sports shop to match the clubs. The shop owner tells him the bag is unique—one of a kind, really. Probably a special order. Dan tells him that his mother bought the set for $125 at a yard sale. The shop owner tells Dan that $125 would not buy even one club in the bag. The shop owner explains that the clubs were tailored for the original owner by a now-defunct company. The original owner was probably exactly Dan's height and weight, which explains why his game has improved. Dan makes a special order of a club style similar to those in the bag, but they will not be an exact match. The shop owner suggests ways to remove the material on the bottom of the bag.

At home, Dan prepares to clean the bag, but receives a duty call, tosses the bag into his trunk, and drives off.

At the station, a team of three detectives meets Dan outside, and they all drive off to the crime scene. Nick, a forensic investigator, places his bag in Dan's trunk, and they drive away.

As the ambulance is being loaded and departs, Dan and Nick return to Dan's car. Placing his bag back in the trunk, Nick notices the dark material on the bottom of the bag. He tells Dan that it looks like blood—human blood—and a lot of it.

They take the bag into the station and put it through a series of tests; they determine that the material is, indeed, human blood. Nick provides some theories as he and Dan talk in a room where the bag, clubs, and the bag's contents are spread out on a large, flat surface. Numerous metal objects reveal fingerprints, and tees and golf balls provide various company logos and markings. They also examine a small towel; a metal cleat tightener; golf cap from a local private club; and one score card listing several rounds for one player—no names, only scores. The blood tests come back, but they are inconclusive due to deterioration of the stains, which may be as much as ten years old.

The forensic team tells Dan that the amount of blood on the bag indicates massive, and perhaps fatal, bleeding occurred. They discuss next steps: police reports of missing people or cold cases from between five and ten years ago; DNA testing on the towel; fingerprint analysis. Nick agrees to take charge of the forensic investigation.

Late at night at his kitchen table, Dan makes notes and reviews photos of the objects that were spread out on the table. He makes a list to retrace steps. Online, he determines that the plant that manufactured the golf clubs burned down five years prior to his discovery of the bag.

It is morning. At the golf store, the owner confirms that without the company records there is no way to trace who purchased the golf clubs.

With his mother, Dan drives through the neighborhood and she recognizes the yard-sale house. Dan knocks on the door. The owners tell him that they recently purchased the house from a widow, who is in a local nursing home.

At city hall, Dan receives information on the house purchase and, back at home, cross-references information on the internet. The widow's husband passed away two years before. His obituary states that he operated a small trash-hauling business in the city for more than thirty years. He is survived by his widow and a son, whom Dan calls.

It is late afternoon. Dan visits the nursing home and finds the widow pleasant and welcoming. He begins to ask probing questions about her husband. She tells him that he was a hoarder who collected everything. One man's trash is another man's treasure. He had a big yard sale every year but liked the stuff too much to sell it—he priced everything way out of the market. Dan probes further, and the widow tells Dan her husband got sick and couldn't take care of himself anymore. When he died, her son had one last big yard sale and sold everything for fifty cents on the dollar. It was all gone in a day.

The widow's son arrives. Dan and the son leave together.

Over coffee, the son tells Dan that he still supervises the business his father started; that it put him through college and funded his MBA; and that it does not create an income for his family, so he has others run the hauling operation. He worked with his dad for much of the last decade. He drove the same defined route, as he was only licensed to go to certain areas in the neighborhood. The son recalls the golf clubs being around for two or three years before his father died. His dad made a big point of having them out every year but had them priced high because someone told him they were worth a lot of money.

The son remembers selling them to Dan's mother; she would not negotiate on the price.

It is a brisk early-fall morning. Dan drives through the neighborhood following a map of the route of the trash haulers. Dog walkers are out and about. Runners and bikers are also about. Construction on a new complex is underway.

Back at the station, Dan's colleagues all have theories and suggestions for next steps, but most feel it is a wild goose chase. Near the end of the meeting, Nick and two other detectives agree to continue to help Dan sort through the evidence again. The investigative team is now five: Dan, Nick, another detective, Vince, and Vanessa—a police officer.

The investigation continues as the team independently reviews evidence. One checks residential records and cross-checks membership at the private club. They find a fingerprint on the golf cleat tool. They follow leads of the logos on the golf balls and tees. A handwriting expert gives a written analysis of the scorecard, noting that the last round is scored through to the eleventh hole. They check the towel for DNA.

A break comes when they determine that three of the members of the private club still live in the neighborhood. One is a recent widow of a banker. One is married with grown children, has an ailing wife, and is a prominent businessman. The third is a widower; his wife passed away seven years ago. With no evidence of a crime, the team discusses strategy going forward. Fingerprints of each of the individuals will be important, as are blood samples.

Late at night at the station, Dan pores over notes and a new outline.

In the morning, Dan visits the first house and greets the banker's widow at her door. Her daughter quickly joins in the conversation and explains that her mother does not remember everything these days. Dan asks the daughter a series of questions that lead him to think that her father may not be a suspect. On the way out of the house through the garage, Dan sees neatly piled boxes and wardrobes of her father's clothes and personal items. Several are marked "Goodwill." A weathered set of golf clubs sits in a monogrammed bag next to the Goodwill items. Back in the car, Dan crosses the widow's name off his list.

Dan drives by the home of the widower, who moves plants in a wheelbarrow from one area to another. Dan parks on the street, walks up to the man, and shows the widower his identification. They take a seat at the patio table, and the man tells Dan about his wife—a prominent doctor in the area. She died of cancer several years before. He has lived alone since then with no family of his own. He talks about dining at the club. Dan asks if the widower plays golf, and the widower says that he had, but gave it up shortly after his wife died. As the conversation winds down, Dan asks if the man could fill his water jug. Dan leaves and, after he is out of sight, pulls over and places the jug in a plastic bag, writing the man's name and the date in marker on the bag.

Back at the team meeting, Dan reports his progress, and confirms the man's story and the wife's death through news reports. After some discussion, the team learns the fingerprints do not match. Dan calls and arranges a time to meet the family of the third club member. The third member has a professional team of handlers, travels frequently, and is hard to pin down. When the family learns that Dan is a detective, they make arrangements to meet him at the private club.

Over lunch, Dan asks many questions, and the third man becomes nervous. He cuts the lunch short and suggests that he and Dan take a ride in a golf cart on the course.

Out on the course, the man confesses that he is concerned that an investigation might affect his business. Dan advises him that would only happen if there were something criminal to investigate. The man admits that he has not been a perfect husband, that his wife has been ill for a long time, and that people could be hurt if the wrong information comes out. He tells Dan that all of it was a long time ago and it really doesn't matter anymore now.

As Dan prods deeper, he learns that the man had an affair with the widower's wife. It ended long before she became ill. He was not able to tell her how much she meant to him before she died. Dan asks about his relationship with the widower. The man confirms all of the stories the widower told him. He tells Dan that everyone at the club knew the widower, and that he used to golf and dine at the club all the time. The man asks Dan if there is anything else. Dan asks him to take him by the eleventh hole.

Dan and the man view the eleventh-hole tee box, drive up the fairway, and walk around the green—a wide, rolling, open area with multiple sand traps.

Back at the station, Dan conducts an internet search. He finds the family records for the man and the widower. The man's story checks out. His wife has suffered from a debilitating condition for most of the last fifteen years. The widower has lived in the area since going to college here—Dan learns he is a native of a nearby village, but there are no records available online.

Dan drives through the village and parks at the village hall. He reviews records with the village clerk. The widower's parents were wealthy landowners, now deceased. He then reviews the birth records and is given one for the widower and one for the widower's twin brother. He goes over news report files in a separate room, and Dan discovers that the twins' parents died in a car crash, that the brothers survived, and that they were raised as wards of the state. Both eventually became successful entrepreneurs. The widower's twin died in a gas explosion at the family plant in town six years earlier. The widower inherited the family wealth.

Dan and the clerk visit the local cemetery and confirm a gravesite for the widower's twin brother.

Arriving home late at night, Dan pulls his car into the driveway and enters his house, visibly weary.

It is sunrise. Dan wakes up late, gathers his papers, and rushes out of the door. Driving quickly through traffic, he is called to a case, but begs out, saying he has something important to do.

Dan arrives at the private club golf course, commandeers a golf cart, and drives to the eleventh green. He reviews the photocopy of the card showing eleven entries. He gets back in the cart and drives to the twelfth tee box. The area is deeply wooded and shady. The sun is blinding, but Dan notices access to the area from the main road. He searches through the brush and walks out across the tee box. He is lost in thought until a foursome arrives at the tee box to play through. Dan watches them drive off the tee, and then he hastily leaves.

At the station, Dan's urgency and tone have changed. He presents a wild scenario about a golfer who keeps his own score on every round that he plays, until one day when he doesn't get to play after making par on the eleventh hole. The team becomes concerned that Dan has crossed the line between the detective and the obsessed. Even his staunch ally Nick has serious doubts. In spite of the evidence, without a body, there is no crime. No fingerprint matches. No criminal records. After more discussion, Dan convinces Nick to do some imaging on the eleventh green and twelfth tee box.

Dan returns home, tired, dejected, and exhausted. He hugs his wife, who consoles him. He falls asleep in his chair with notes, photos, and other paperwork scattered around him.

It is early morning. Dan joins his family at the breakfast table. He is unkempt from lack of sleep. His daughter worries about her father. Dan's cell phone rings. Forensics has found something near the twelfth tee.

A growing number of law enforcement personnel gather at the twelfth tee box. A metal detector has discovered two long objects buried in the area adjacent to the box. As Dan arrives, the team discovers two mangled golf clubs—a driver and a five iron—in a two-foot-deep hole.

They cordon off the area, now a suspected crime scene, as forensic investigators begin to move in. Police divert golfers away from the area. They close the club and seal the area. Dan and the investigator watch as the team uncovers a decomposed body in a shallow grave near the tee box.

The preliminary report, provided to the chief and precinct attorneys, finds the victim is a man in his sixties. Before sending the report, Dan confirms the man's height and weight. They find, buried with the body, a money clip that has a fingerprint.

It is dusk. Dan arrives at the widower's home. He rings the bell and the widower answers the door. The widower is surprised to see Dan. Dan enters and notices the television is on with news of the unexplained police activity at the club. There has been no public announcement of the investigation, but helicopters hover over the twelfth hole, and reporters interview club members outside the clubhouse. The widower and Dan settle into chairs.

Dan asks the widower if he knows why he is there. The widower says that he has an idea that somehow Dan believes that he may have done something wrong.

Dan lays out a story of two twin brothers, one depressed, lonely, and despondent after the death of his wife, and the other in financial crisis in a business that's sucking the family wealth dry. The brothers plot together to fake a death, and the resulting insurance and family inheritance will support them in a lavish way for the rest of their lives. The only problem is that they must live one life—one identical life—in a small town where no one can know.

Dan says the plan worked well for a while—private-club living, golf, and travel. With two cars, they could leave and spend long periods apart paying with cash. But eventually, with the development of technology, it would have to come to an end. One of the brothers would be jealous of the life of the other. Only one could ultimately survive.

It all came to an end on the twelfth tee early one morning. Knowing just where he would be, one brother killed the other, buried the evidence, and returned to the relative peace and quiet of his neighborhood. One question remains: Which twin was the golfer?

The widower tells Dan that he was always jealous of his brother. When their parents died, his brother got most of the attention because he got banged up pretty bad. His brother also knew the accident was his twin's fault, he says. He had distracted his father and caused him to run off the road.

"We kept that secret all our lives," he tells Dan. "My brother worked hard for everything he got, and life came easy for him. He fell in love and had a wonderfully successful and beautiful wife. I admired her. I loved her. I think that she loved me, and that used to infuriate him. He thought we were having an affair, but we weren't. The stress got to her and she got sick. He needed to take care of her, but she didn't want him around. She wanted me. He was despondent . . . lost . . . shaken. So we hatched the plan, and it was glorious fun at first. The explosion . . . the secrecy . . . and my brother was happy to have the help. I took care of his wife until the day she died. No one knew I was here. After she died, he had great remorse—survivor's guilt. He grew depressed, and I was concerned it would all unravel. He had such a good life and was wasting it away, so I decided he was better off where he is. I wanted that life so much I was willing to kill him for it. He never knew what hit him."

Dan pauses for a moment to take in all that he has heard. He rises and walks to the door as police officers enter to arrest the twin brother of the widower.

"They will throw the book at you, you know?" Dan says, as he pauses at the door.

The twin brother yells "FORE!" as the officers handcuff him and lead him out of the house.

THE END

Act II, Scene 1

She's a fine old girl she is.
Don't be sayin' she's not cuz she is.
And we'll stay by her side cuz
you won't recognize us
When we pop the lot of you
just at the thought of you
Tellin' us get on our way
That this charmer has seen her best day.
She's a fine old girl, she is.
Don't be sayin' she's not cuz she is!

The Window Washers
Act II, Scene 1

ACT II, SCENE 1

SETTING: Exterior Urban Office Building and
            Street Scene
            Six Months Later—Gray Overcast/Nearly
            Spring

SONGS: SHE'S A FINE OLD GIRL, SHE IS
            ALL GOOD THINGS (THAT WE HAD)
            ALL GOOD THINGS (GOIN' BAD)

AT RISE: Midmorning. A pair of window washers are
            suspended on individual lines against
            the exterior of the building, which has
            lost its luster from the opening scene.

Two washers appear on the street below and two others
on the roof. The washers all sing SHE'S A FINE OLD
GIRL, SHE IS as they clean and dance suspended on the
exterior of the building. The street-level washers
enter the building as the façade gives way to the
lobby area.

The lobby is under repair. Outrageous sponsored
signage of all kinds fills the space: a larger-
than-life-sized cutout of the CHIEF with a "LEAVE

IT TO US!" thought bubble, logos, and mismatched rah-rah slogans. All washers converge in the lobby, transitioning into painters and paperhangers. Scaffolding is visible, lights hang from the ceiling, and temporary repairs are underway. Confused patients jam the lobby, waiting for the elevator—including the IMPATIENT PATIENT, seated in a wheelchair nearby with the ORDERLY. JOE and the CHAOSALS are present and observing.

TESS, TOSS, and MOTHER emerge from the chaos and lead the COMPANY in ALL GOOD THINGS (THAT WE HAD). As the CHAOSALS create more havoc, JOE sings ALL GOOD THINGS (GOIN' BAD). The action culminates in the COMPANY completing the musical number.

The CHIEF enters with architects to discuss renovation of the gift shop. MOTHER overhears the plans and an argument ensues. TESS and TOSS complain about the structural, heat, and ventilation problems. An assistant shows some of the merchandise that will be for sale. The IMPATIENT PATIENT gets involved, then, with his cane, strikes at, but misses, the ORDERLY.

The CHIEF guides architects to another area and all exit. The CHAOSALS open windows that let in a blast of frigid air. Shorted-out lights dangling from their bases begin to flicker. Plaster begins to fall, the walls buckle, and the COMPANY nervously exits—except for JOE, the CHAOSALS, the IMPATIENT PATIENT, and the ORDERLY.

JOE motions upward. The lights flicker again, and as JOE and the CHAOSALS begin to exit, the lobby magically restores itself more or less to normal.

The reversal is not immediately apparent to the
IMPATIENT PATIENT and the ORDERLY as they have
been busy looking at the merchandise. Once the
transformation is complete, they hurriedly exit.

BLACKOUT

CHAPTER 38

PERIPHERAL NEUROPATHY AND VIV

Dear Mark,

Let's have a chat!

As you know, for most of the last year it has been a challenge to perform at the level that I have been used to because the treatments I received caused a weariness that is unexplainable—a feeling that does not come from physical exhaustion but somewhere else. And, hard as you try, you cannot sleep your way out of it.

Chemotherapy ended in January 2009, and as I write this in May, I have been working at roughly the same pace for most of the last couple of months with good energy, clear thoughts, and moderate to high productivity. The one challenge I face is the enormous amount of writing and typing that I have in my job. As an adjustment, I tend to write short responses to everyone in email and have been trying to repurpose a lot of my work to save time and energy, and to increase effectiveness.

I've felt for some time, however, that I've not been fair to those people who have done so much to make areas of our operation successful. Most of that recognition would come from me in the form of a letter, email, or just a note. I have been good at this most of my professional career, but now I find the process of writing arduously difficult and typing to be frustrating on good days—and virtually impossible on bad days.

I have developed a painful condition called peripheral neuropathy as a result of one of the medications I took during my chemotherapy sessions. Neuropathy is the tingly feeling you have in your hands and feet when they "fall asleep," except it is now a constant in my life. Bothersome virtually all the time, unexplained flares come and go on the bad days, which can be incapacitating.

I have always been a hunt-and-peck typist, so this situation has really hampered my ability. These days, I find it hard to keep up with the volume of typing, text messaging, and other forms of written communication that exist. I need to conserve my energy and be more selective along the way.

And then . . . along came MacSpeech!

Late last year, I purchased this product for my personal writing. I found it to be extremely helpful in script development for the television program I produce and host at the Pritzker Military Library and also for other major writing projects. I just said that previous sentence, and MacSpeech typed it on the page. What technology!

I started training my new voice-recognition friend, VRF, or "Viv," to type every sentence almost perfectly. Soon, I was writing massive background pieces, notes for interviews, scripts, and letters that were almost better than my feeble typing could be. It also worked with email, so I could reply to email concisely and with more detail and nuance than a conventionally typed reply.

I was ecstatic!

One night, while I was in the middle of my home treatment and after a particularly exhausting research session on an interview topic, Denise came home to find me slumped over the kitchen table asleep at my Mac. Viv was still bravely typing whatever she had heard for the last hour, which looked a lot like snoring on each of the twenty-four pages on the screen.

zzzzzzzzhhhhhzzzzhzhzzzzhhzzzhhzzzhzhzhzzzzzz . . .

I thought that once chemotherapy was over and I started feeling better, I would have no further need for my speech-recognition program. However, the neuropathy has become more intense in the last couple of months—a sort of phantom effect. After seeking the advice of a neurologist, I was told that while many see the effects dissipate over time, there is no known cure for a small percentage of patients. The neurologist gave me some other medications for this condition, but they have side effects, so I have tried to maintain my workload around other kinds of pain medication that help to relieve symptoms of the condition.

Virtually everything I have written here was first produced with Viv. I think, someday, Viv might be helpful in choosing a fishing fly or just the right club for a long uphill approach shot to a green.

During massage-therapy sessions, I regained about 90 percent of the feeling in my hands. The numbness I feel in my feet is still debilitating. I move around in a clumsy and awkward fashion, stumbling and falling sometimes. I hold onto a rail going down stairs like a much older person. It feels like this part will not go away any time soon.

Time will tell, but at this stage, I am happy that Viv can help me keep writing and communicating every day—even if, once in a while, I run out of gas and can sleep sitting up.

MAY 9, 2009

CHAPTER 39

DEAR JOHN—ADVENTURES

Dear John,

I have been thinking a lot today about adventures.

We seem to spend time, energy, and resources so that we can escape the everyday nature of life for a spot unknown. A good, old-fashioned adventure. Exciting new surroundings. A different culture, cuisine, climate. A place where everything is new and just about anything can happen.

Why do we need this escape from reality? What are we looking for? What should we do when we find it?

It could be our upbringing. Perhaps our parents instilled in us the promise of an adventurous life—to live outside our own boundaries as often as possible. They might have let us know what it felt like to dream of these destinations from time to time growing up.

And then there is the active imagination of youth, fueled by books, magazines, films, and the storytellers of our youth who talked about seeing the world. Today, the internet and social media do the same.

Most of us exist in the wide divide between what keeps us close to home and what pushes us to parts unknown. Until we are on the road to an adventure, whether it is up a mountain or across another continent, modern technology may allow us to experience what it feels like to sail the Atlantic or soar like an eagle high over the Andes.

Nothing compares to the real thing.

So, why do we submit ourselves to airport security, travel delays, various modes of transportation, and the inconvenience of hotels where reality does not match the marketing materials aimed at those who seek relaxation?

For the adventure of it all.

Throughout the 1980s and 1990s, I traveled extensively for business and was ready to park my road-warrior persona. I made a commitment when I moved back to Vermont in 1989 to live within a mile from where I worked for the rest of my life.

These days, of course, that means working from home.

As the years in Vermont passed and I became content to live and work this way, the urge to be more adventurous took hold. As wonderful as Vermont can be, fishing on big western rivers became a priority, which in turn made returning to the sidewalks and show palaces of New York City invigorating. Times Square became familiar territory, accessible, and, in a comforting way, it felt like home whenever I lounged at the second-floor bar at Sardi's watching the bustle on West Forty-Fourth Street leading up to an 8 p.m. curtain.

But real adventures require wilderness. So, I started taking expeditions close to home, at first. Hiking the Long Trail. Climbing Mount Washington. Searching for the largest lobster in Maine, the best fried clams outside of Cape Cod, and the freshest corn on the cob that was right in my own garden.

I always traveled with at least one other person, but then a group of anglers inducted me into their own storied adventure group, the Order of the Ancient Fishermen's Society, or OAFS as they are known. In my first year, I was designated a lower OAF, or LOAF. It was all good fun, and I am not sure when I actually became a bona fide OAF. (In truth, I have seen only a few LOAFs come and go from this group, so it is a lifetime appointment.)

On the Hudson float trip, my first, we camped by the river, ran out of our four-day supply of scotch on day two, and landed shimmering native rainbows at every turn. I suffered severe burns on both hands that made holding the steering wheel nearly impossible on the drive home. I would never fish again without gloves on both hands.

Later excursions to Wyoming, Maine, Belize, and New Brunswick were grand opportunities to diversify our equipment for larger and ever-more-challenging fish. Each was an exploration of our personal limits and skill, but none compared to the midsummer 2008 trip to Umiakovik Lake in Labrador.

Labrador is three-quarters of the way to Greenland, or so I was told. Umiakovik is accessible by land in the wintertime by snowmobile. The lake is ice-free from July 15 through October 15 and available for guided trips for only six weeks during that period. The lake is home to an enormous population of Arctic char, a species coined the "grandfather of all trout" that averages between three to five pounds.

Our five-day trip insured privacy, adventure, and a fishing experience of a lifetime. We began planning and paid a year in advance to secure our spot in a tight six-week schedule that is routinely impacted by unpredictable weather patterns, and with the added challenge of packing and planning for a weight-limited single-engine high-wing de Havilland Canada DHC-2 Beaver float plane that would transport four anglers, a pilot, equipment, and supplies over a steep mountain system. We would be isolated from all outside contact except by shortwave radio.

There were lots of challenges on this adventure.

One of them was me.

Everything was on track for our OAF adventure until I was diagnosed with stage 3C colon cancer on June 30. With only six weeks until takeoff, the diagnosis, surgery, and initial chemotherapy treatment seriously threatened any chance that I would be able to go.

With my doctor's consent, I set out to get back into shape. I walked every day following my surgery as I prepared for the first round of chemotherapy. The ever-expanding walking route eventually led me to the local Orvis store where I compared various lines and flies I was researching with the real thing.

The treatment would surely impact my energy level leading up to departure, but I decided if I could travel on the first weekend following treatment, I could bounce back and finish the trip in reasonable shape for the second treatment.

I should say at this point that no one, including my OAF brethren, thought the trip was a good idea. It was extremely high risk in my condition. I was going to the wilderness, away from everything.

So, off I went. All of the excitement and anticipation, my trusted 7-weight Orvis fly rod in hand, loaded with gear and ready to join the merry band of OAFS for the adventure of a lifetime—a week in a lakeside hut on the remote, sandy shore of Umiakovik in search of peace, tranquility, and the elusive Arctic char.

Reality set in right from the beginning. I could barely push my cart through the terminal to the international gate. I had help along the way, but I realized immediately that the effects of the treatment were severe. I was traveling alone and had not been in a crowd for weeks. I had not factored in that my resistance to infection was dangerously low, so I avoided contact.

Everywhere I turned, travelers looked on with sadness in their eyes. I was just trying to get to the next destination, but I was not smiling and must have looked pretty ashen and miserable. I thought seriously of turning back. I wanted to take a nap, but I pulled down my cap, put on sunglasses, and pretended I was invisible.

On the plane to Montreal, I dozed the catatonic sleep you get when you are on chemotherapy. Someone told me in advance that it is a tired and weary feeling that cannot be satisfied with rest or sleep. I longed for the days when I could work or play hard, and then get that restful, energizing sleep that rejuvenates. Those days were behind me for the time being.

Upon arrival, the OAFS were to meet at a hotel near the airport. I navigated my gear bags and rods to the street, waited in line, and eventually took a cab to the wrong hotel. After a second cab ride, I arrived, checked into the room, and collapsed in bed—unable to move, unable to sleep, dehydrated, and feeling sick. I had a few hours to pull myself together before the rest of the group arrived. I was hopeful I'd bounce back.

At this juncture, I should say that six weeks after abdominal surgery, your stitches are still in place. Core strength I might have had previously was nonexistent. I was advised not to lift anything heavier than fifteen pounds. I had been on a diet of protein, lots of fish, rice, and mashed vegetables with lots of water. I drank diluted Gatorade for the electrolytes.

So when the OAFS gathered around me in my room, it was reminiscent of Dorothy's last scene in *The Wizard of Oz*. I looked up at each one of them, and they knew that I had just gone through a stressful ordeal, but they didn't let on. They encouraged me to go out for a few last-minute supplies, but I begged off and agreed to meet everyone for dinner.

Although I was not a fascinating conversationalist that evening, I felt better. Being in the company of the OAFS had a lot to do with it.

The next day, we boarded a flight to Schefferville, Quebec, home to Montagnais Innu Nation on the border of Labrador. The stop was the pathway to Umiakovik, the final destination several hours north. We were to hold in place for twelve to twenty-four hours until the weather pattern allowed a safe flight over the mountains into camp. It was critical to time our flight in such a way that the outgoing group could safely return in the same six-hour period.

Our hold in place turned into two days, and without much to do there, the delay taxed everyone. Not moving for two days was a positive turn for me. The effects of the first treatment were dissipating, and now I was getting as eager as the rest to continue.

Once airborne, we experienced cramped conditions, the constant roar of the engine, and severe wind gusts navigated masterfully by our pilot/tour manager. The terrain below turned into a stunning moonscape—scant vegetation, shrubs, glacial peaks, and rocky shores along endless waterways.

Our approach to Umiakovik was awe-inspiring. Rugged, jutting rock cliffs encircled a pristine lake against an endless and shimmering horizon. We could see a sandy shoreline and a group of small outbuildings as the plane tipped toward the lake to land perfectly and taxi to the shore.

The exiting group stood in a line to greet us, bags packed, eager— it appeared—to depart. In our short exchange as we gathered our gear on the beach, the group told us that the weather had been great, the food was good, the fish took only one particular fly, and that they had shot a bear the night before.

A bear.

Did I hear that right? Should we be worried? No one had mentioned the presence of bears up to this point. I was still shaken from the plane ride: ears ringing, nauseated. And now, there was a bear.

One of OAFS said there was nothing to worry about: the bear was dead.

That's when the guide chimed in, "Well, actually, fellas, this particular bear, and his mate, have been seen around camp a lot."

The same astonished look flashed across the face of each of the OAFS.

"Let's just say," the guide continued, "that if you have to whiz in the middle of the night, look out the little window of your cabin before you go."

He assured us that if the bear came back, the guide was loaded up and ready for him. Somehow, that did not comfort us.

We unpacked and all regrouped in the meeting house for lunch. Our superb cook and baker, Sally, was a forty-year-old woman who kept to herself for most of the time we were there. She had been in camp for more than a month and didn't socialize with guests.

After lunch, I wanted to retire for a nap. I knew that I would not sleep, but now that we had arrived at our destination, I felt like I needed time to recalibrate.

At this point, the OAFS took over. In truth, they had been carrying my bags from the moment we met at the hotel, anticipating my needs and helping me at every turn. They have never admitted it, but I sense that they all got together before dinner that first night and decided how they were going to get me out and back safely. They were very patient with me, which made all the difference.

Now they banded together and redirected me to the water. They made a strong case for completing our adventure in the next hour, gearing up and heading to the lake for Arctic char. Each one was eager to cast a fly on the lake, and they were not going to do it without me.

So, we all geared up and, together, took the walk with the guide to the inlet where the water flowed from a smaller tributary into the lake. It was at this juncture that the colder water fed in and scores of char hovered adjacent to the shore.

On this day, Umiakovik had gentle three-foot waves and smaller ripples surging against the shore. The guide instructed us to fan out into separate locations and suggested that the best spot might be near the intersection of the water flow to the lake. I was set up on a safe, easy access point on the rocky beach.

From my position, I could see directly through the cone formed as the waves came toward the shore, and I spotted dozens of char suspended, almost as if frozen, in place. As I looked down the column of water, char kept rising up, parallel to the shore, holding in position for a moment, glistening in the afternoon sun.

The guide leaned in over my shoulder and pointed to a stretch in which to cast, just ahead of the ripples as the char emerged inside the cone. Casting into the column, I immediately had a strike. The fish bolted straight out of the water as I adjusted the drag, and then took off like a rocket away from the shore, my reel singing loudly, the 7-weight rod bent gloriously in the direction of the fish.

The OAFS had yet to cast. In fact, I think they watched as I reeled in a two-pound char.

In all of the planning, I had not factored in the pull weight of wild char. I'd estimate a two to three-pound char has a pull weight in the area of fifteen to twenty pounds. Since I was not supposed to lift anything heavier than fifteen pounds, the landing of just one fish could pose problems.

What occurred, however, was magical. On the next dozen casts, I landed eight fish—at one point landing three in a row. The OAFS sadly had no luck at all. So I traded places, each time reading the water column and casting into the cone. The fish kept coming no matter what position I was in. Adrenaline coursed through my body.

I was euphoric and alive. And I probably cumulatively bench-pressed about 150 pounds in that hour.

It turned out that we were short of food supplies for one meal and some of my catch became the next night's meal. In a moment of enormous personal pride for me, Sally brought a heaping platter of golden panfried char to the table and said, "I think it's safe to say that Ed caught dinner tonight, boys."

In all the OAF adventures, I rarely caught the most fish or the largest, but this particular day on Umiakovik would never be equaled.

That night, at 3 a.m. when nature called, I looked out the window at the moon-swept lake and saw the silhouette of a bear lumbering by the cabin about twenty feet away.

When I tried to rouse my bunkmate, he said, "Take a picture," and then nodded off back to sleep. After ten tense minutes, I made a dash to and from the latrine without another sighting, which was confirmed in the morning by the tracks at the shore.

My luck continued for two days until my rod broke, and the painful reality set in that my stitches had been compromised, which sidelined me for good. In the quiet and reflective time that followed, I made the decision that I would propose to Denise when I returned, and then I announced my decision to the OAFS so I could not change my mind.

We seem to spend time, energy, and resources so that we can escape the everyday nature of life for a spot unknown. A good old-

fashioned adventure. Exciting new surroundings. A different culture, cuisine, climate. A place where everything is new and just about anything can happen.

That place is not all that far away. It is found in shared memories in the company of lifelong friends and by surrounding yourself with those you love.

Tight Lines!

JUNE 27, 2015

CHAPTER 40

PEOPLE I KNEW —FOR ANN TURNER, WITH LOVE

I WILL ALWAYS CHERISH two of three gifts Ann Turner gave to me: a tattered paperback and a handwritten note—precious memories from a person who was all at once a mentor, coach, teacher, editor, scholar, cheerleader, wife, mother, caretaker, and friend.

Ann Turner was a one-of-a-kind human being who displayed a sense of presence—the art of living in the moment. Never doubt that behind her quiet and engaging personality, there existed a keen judge of character, comparing and contrasting what she saw and heard to any one of the great works of literature she loved.

After interacting with generations of students, alumni, faculty, and staff at Norwich, Ann began spending more time with George, bustling around the countryside, playing golf on early summer mornings, hosting functions, attending sporting events, and traveling for family and friends' celebrations. Ann inspired everyone to make reading a priority in their lives. Together, just about everywhere they went, George and AJ were the life of every party.

One of my weekly rituals was to stop by for a visit—to listen, learn, ask for advice, get talked off a ledge, hear a new song, and, many times, share a pizza, grilled cheese, or shrimp cocktail. It was never formal, but oh what a swell party it was.

After moving to Chicago, our weekly conversations continued on the phone or by email. We exchanged books and debated projects, and a delightful repartee emerged. When Ann answered the phone, I'd ask, "Is this the incredible Ann Turner?" She would say, "This is the incredible one herself!" Every so often, I would change it up with other adjectives from my thesaurus, including "amazing," "lovely," "captivating," and a particular favorite, "ebullient!" Each time, the same wonderfully warm conversation would eventually be passed along to George when Ann would say that "our wandering boy from Chicago" was on the phone. I am reasonably convinced that I was not the only "wandering boy" in the Turner universe, but they always made me feel that way.

I learned to listen from Ann Turner. She was an active listener, making astute correlations to topics, expressing spot-on opinions and commentary, and revealing her unique brand of humor in every situation. She would lean in when she talked to you and look you straight in the eye. And then her crafty, knowing, lovely smile would fill the room.

At no time was this more apparent than one of the last times I visited Winter Street during a brief trip from Chicago. George regaled us with a story that I might have heard a few times before. In the next moment, he stopped abruptly and then struggled to recall a name that was familiar to us. As I started to complete the sentence, Ann said softly, "He'll get it. Give him time." And, of course, he did, but something became clear in that moment: I realized the two people whose love and support had meant so much to me were mortal.

George passed on Thursday, October 8, 2009. I arrived at Winter Street on Saturday. All of the family gathered in support, as they had done for several months. Throughout that day and evening, Ann and I sat together and talked off and on. There were long moments of silence, and then things would come around again to past stories, trips, and literature. George and Ann had been early and enthusiastic supporters of the Colby Symposium. It had been important to George on so many levels to bring Phil Caputo and Bill Colby together on stage for the first program in 1995. I never truly understood why at the time, but George was passionate, and so was Ann. She told me that she saw the life lessons that each of the writers could bring to Norwich students. She was pleased that the program promised to help place military literature front and center for students and the community.

The next day, Ann quietly left the living room for a time and returned with a tattered paperback copy of Phil Caputo's *A Rumor of War*. It was heavily annotated and stuffed with lecture notes from different classes on the topic that George had taught. There were program materials from our first symposium inside, along with a copy of a Norwich Record obituary that George had written honoring Walt Levy, a student of his and the first Norwich graduate to die in Vietnam.

Later in the afternoon, we took a ride to nowhere, over mountains bursting with fall color, in search of a general store that sold Vermont cheddar cheese—a clever ruse to get her out of the house. We talked a bit, but at some point near Sugarbush, Ann settled back in her seat and fell into a deep and restful sleep. She was so quiet that when we returned to Winter Street, I sat parked in the car with her for another fifteen minutes before I woke her.

A few weeks later, Ann wrote a short note, which I now keep in a special place, along with George's copy of *A Rumor of War*.

It read simply:

> Dear Ed,
>
> I want to thank you for staying with me during the worst day.
>
> Love,
> Ann

Two of the three gifts from Ann Turner that I will always cherish are a tattered paperback and a handwritten note.

The third is her unconditional love.

The Wandering Boy (from Chicago)

Act II, Scene 2

Standing outside the door and wondering
What's in store today.
Friends drop by
and call with a sigh
Not truly saying
the thoughts they are saving.
Sad. Confused. Not knowing what to do.
They're saying
"How is he?" "How's he doing?"
"This will all be over and he'll be home
soon."
And all I can say, when I
catch my breath
"How is he?
"What about me?"

Katharine
Act II Scene 2

ACT II, SCENE 2

SETTING: Waiting Room

SONGS: HOW IS HE (WHAT ABOUT ME)
             HOME/HOLIDAYS

AT RISE: CLINT, KATHARINE, JIM and MEGAN sit in
             the waiting room as the elevator doors
             open.

More patients and the IMPATIENT PATIENT enter.
KATHARINE leads HOW IS HE (WHAT ABOUT ME).

NAN directs CLINT, JILL, and MEGAN to the treatment
room as SAM and JACK enter. JACK concludes the song
with KATHARINE.

KATHARINE is hopeful, animated and excited.

Despite these efforts, SAM is detached and steps
out of the scene and into a flashback—a previous
conversation with THOMPSON.

SAM and THOMPSON sing HOME/HOLIDAYS.

THOMPSON exits.

SAM steps back into the scene with KATHARINE.
As he begins to tell her the diagnosis,

                    LIGHTS FADE TO BLACK

CHAPTER 42

MAKING CHEMO CONNECTIONS

MY FIRST SESSION WAS made easier by a longtime friend of Denise's who works in the chemo ward. I should also probably explain at this point that in Chicago, and virtually everywhere I have traveled with Denise over the last four years, she knows someone, or someone recognizes her. She is just one of those people. And in the chemo ward, there are lots of friendly faces on staff, but knowing even one person personally there gave us both an edge in dealing with what was to come. That was a pleasant and wonderful surprise, as it always is when Denise makes the connection.

The chemo ward is a large, sunlit room with more than thirty comfortable, blue reclining chairs. My treatments last about five hours and involve a series of several separate doses that attack different elements of the disease at various stages in their growth cycle. (I'll probably have to ask my oncologist to edit that last statement, so if it now sounds like more than a simple description, you know that he helped me out.) Along the way, they also provide anti-nausea medicine and an array of pills for whatever else might affect me as result of the actual medical treatment.

I was surprised to learn that I can eat, read, email, talk quietly on the phone, and do just about anything else while receiving my treatment.

The third drug causes a cold feeling.

One made me sleepy.

Trips to the bathroom with my little rolling chemo bag hanger are a frequent interruption. That room is under heavy demand when the ward is full, and, from time to time, competition to get there keen.

Following the formal treatment, I am fitted with a portable pump that I wear for another thirty-six hours. The pump is the size of an old Walkman and straps around the waist with a clip belt. On my treatment plan, I'll be out of commission for a few days in the middle. Surprisingly, I can function quite well day to day with the pump attached. I am sure that the array of steroids and other drugs involved make me feel better, because I have found that during this period, my energy is good; I work regular hours; and I can hide the pump under the oversized clothes I still have in the closet.

And on the last day of treatment, the pump signals the end, and I remove the apparatus from my port-a-cath all by myself. It is a liberating feeling. I celebrate with a hot shower.

I made the fishing trip, but I would not recommend it a few days after anyone's first chemotherapy treatment. My three fishing buddies—all ten years my senior—carried the sack for me all the way to Labrador. I will never forget their kindness, or that they allowed me to catch more than twenty char on the first day. The trip stressed most of the stitches and delayed my physical recovery by several weeks, but it did wonders for my head and heart to be there in the wilderness.

On that isolated trip, I decided to propose to Denise. We are to be married on New Year's Eve. And yes, I lost thirty pounds along the way here, so the wardrobe I outgrew two years ago has suddenly come back into my life. I went back to work and back into production the week after Labor Day, six weeks after surgery.

OCTOBER 2008

CHAPTER 43

PEOPLE I KNEW— WERNER KLEMPERER— RARE TUNA

SOME PEOPLE SAY THAT you need to make your own luck. I'd rather think that what we perceive as luck in life is really the combination of inspiration, passion, and the kindness of strangers all intersecting at a precise moment.

Our conversations always began something like this:

"Hello," I would say.

Werner Klemperer's voice on the other end of the line was distinctive, raw and dynamic.

"Driver! How the [expletive] hell are you?"

"Werner," I said to the man who was known as Colonel Klink on the 1960s television show *Hogan's Heroes,* and who was the son of the world-famous conductor Otto Klemperer. "Great to hear your voice. How are you?"

"The whole world is going to [expletive] shit, but what else is [expletive] new?"

Lots of expletives filled any conversation with Werner Klemperer, but he was always warm, and friendly, and the rest just seemed to spew out naturally—almost matter-of-factly. I am sure that those closest to him heard more of the same playful banter that I did on his calls.

Werner started referring to me as "Driver" during the 1997 Parent/Family Weekend appearance that he and his wife, Kim Hamilton, attended at Norwich University. I don't recall him once calling me by my name. It would have seemed awkward if he had.

Werner and Kim were introduced to Norwich a year before at Sardi's Restaurant in New York City when our mutual friend and restaurant owner Vincent Sardi invited the couple to be special guests at one of our "Norwich Night on Broadway" events.

The reception and dinner preceded a performance that evening of *A Funny Thing Happened on the Way to the Forum,* starring Nathan Lane. It was memorialized in a superb photo from the reception with trustee and 1959 Norwich alum retired US Army general Gordon R. Sullivan; retired US Coast Guard rear admiral Richard W. Schneider, president of Norwich University; and, of course, Colonel Klink.

Werner once told me that Klink's monocle—a prized artifact from the show—had been stolen and never replaced. So, after his remarks to the group, I presented him with an elegant eyeglass magnifier that looked much like the famous monocle as a gift. When he raised it to his eye, Werner reverted immediately to Klink, playfully giving me some orders before grabbing my head in his massive hands and kissing me square on the lips.

Werner knew his audience.

In the mid-1990s, it was hard to imagine that a television show about a bumbling Nazi prison-camp commandant and US prisoners single-handedly winning the war had ever made it to television. It was a regular question that Werner fielded effortlessly as a sign of the time in interviews.

He was much more candid in private.

"It was a [expletive] TV show, for Christ's sake!" he told me. "And it plays in syndication all over the world, including in Germany since 1992. Everyone knew we were making a [expletive] farce, and it was a hit!" he said, adding, "John Banner [Schultz] was a lovely, lovely man. Just like you see him on the show."

Decades after the show premiered, Norwich University's Corps of Cadets marched to the *Hogan's Heroes* theme song. But as times and attitudes changed, they dropped it in the early 1990s in favor of a more traditional military march.

By the time the 1997 Parents/Family Weekend rolled around, the significance of the television theme song was a distant memory.

After Werner and Kim addressed a standing-room-only talk for parents and students about their careers, they joined the Sardis and rode onto Sabine Field during halftime of the football game in an Army jeep. Werner, who had appeared with many of the finest orchestras in the world as guest orator and conductor, took the baton from director Jim Bennett, stepped to the podium, and conducted the Norwich Band in what may have been the final performance ever of the *Hogan's Heroes* theme.

Following the game, I invited the group to my log cabin for cocktails before dinner that evening at a nearby restaurant. It was then that Werner noticed a large collection of books on the life and career of Buster Keaton. I told him that I had been working on a musical treatment of Buster's life, had outlined the story, written a few songs, and was in the process of putting the show together.

Werner was interested. He pulled up a chair next to the piano and asked me to play some of the music on the spot. I offered to play a couple of recordings, but he insisted on hearing the songs live.

"What the [expletive] are you afraid of?" he said. "We're all friends here."

So, I nervously sat down at the piano and played—and sang—three songs from the show with a brief commentary to set the scene for each one. I gained confidence as my fifteen-minute impromptu performance progressed, but not enough to feel at all comfortable.

When I finished, Werner looked at me and said, "That's very nice. I think I may know someone who could help you."

And with that as the final word, we took the short ride to a new restaurant for dinner.

I had not identified our guests in advance on Vincent's advice. He was more at ease without preferential treatment at local restaurants and wanted to avoid any issues that might arise from Werner's popularity. It was going to be a quiet, friendly dinner after a long day.

We were seated in a secluded area of the restaurant at a large table and assigned a waiter in his late teens who welcomed us to the new restaurant's—and his—first Saturday night.

After drinks were served, the waiter began to take entrée orders from steak and chops to seafood.

Hovering over his menu, Werner asked about the tuna.

"The tuna is very fine, sir," the waiter said.

"I have found," Werner said, "that for tuna to be exceptional, it must be served very, very rare. Can you do that?"

"Yes, sir," the waiter said, making a big note on his pad as he said, "Very, very rare."

"That will be fine," Werner said. "Thank you."

When the waiter left, Werner expounded on his views about tuna, and the many places he had been served the dish around the world, and then complimented Vincent on the glorious dining experience that he always had at Sardi's. The conversation drifted off to other topics over salads and more wine until the table was cleared for the main course.

The waiter began to serve everyone else before Werner. As he placed the entrée on the table, all eyes turned to Werner, who stared down in disbelief.

There, placed mournfully in the center of the plate, was a small, charred mass that looked more like a scorched piece of beef than fish.

Werner crossed his hands at the edge of the table, still looking down at the plate, his thumbs pressing together as if to pump the next words that he was about to say.

"Excuse me," Werner said. "Is this the tuna?"

"Yes, sir," the waiter said nervously.

"Does this look like rare tuna to you?" Werner continued.

"Ah, yes?" the waiter said, not at all confidently.

Sitting back in his chair, crossing his arms and looking directly at the waiter, Werner asked quizzically, "Would YOU eat this?"

It was then that things took an ominous turn.

The waiter, thinking that Werner was directing him, picked up a fork, hacked off a piece of the tuna and took a big bite.

I wanted to crawl under the table. Everyone else looked on in astonishment.

Werner, however, remained still, calmly watching as the waiter chewed and then swallowed what must have been a very dry mouthful of tuna.

"So," Werner said. "How was it?"

"I don't know," the waiter said. "I don't like tuna."

Our conversation a few days later began something like this:

"Hello," I said.

Werner Klemperer's voice on the other end of the line was distinctive, raw, and dynamic.

"Driver! How the [expletive] hell are you?"

"Werner," I said. "Great to hear your voice. How are you?"

"The whole world is going to [expletive] shit, but what else is [expletive] new?" Werner said. "And I have told a hundred people about the rare tuna story."

"Destined to be a classic," I said.

"I am sure he meant well, the little [expletive][expletive]! Say, Driver," Werner continued. "I have someone I'd like you to call. His name is Jimmy Karen and he has been a friend of Buster's forever. I just got off the phone with him and told him about your project. He said to give him a call. Here's the number."

Within an hour, I was speaking with the renowned film and television character actor James Karen, who in the next hour put me in touch with Buster's widow, Eleanor Keaton, which began an unforgettable yearlong friendship—a breakthrough moment for the project.

Some people say that you need to make your own luck. I'd rather think that what we perceive as luck in life is really the combination of inspiration, passion and the kindness of strangers all intersecting at a precise moment.

CHAPTER 44

A LETTER FOR KIM HAMILTON

January 9, 2014

Cheryl Boone Isaacs
President
Academy of Motion Picture Arts and Sciences
8949 Wilshire Boulevard
Beverly Hills, California 90211

Dear Ms. Isaacs,

The Academy has a unique opportunity, during this year's awards ceremony, to acknowledge in memoriam the career of Kim Hamilton, an extraordinary actress who passed away on September 16, 2013, at the age of eighty-one.

In a career that spanned more than six decades, Ms. Hamilton appeared as Brock Peters' wife in *To Kill a Mockingbird*, and as the wife of Harry Belafonte in *Odds Against Tomorrow*. Other memorable film credits include *The Greatest Story Ever Told*, *Body and Soul*, *The Wild Angels*, and the cult film *Leach Women*. Ms. Hamilton most recently appeared in the 2010 film *The Beginners*.

Ms. Hamilton's long television career includes dozens of featured appearances, from Andy's girlfriend on *Amos & Andy* to roles in *All in the Family*, *The Jeffersons*, and *Star Trek: The Next Generation*, as well as numerous soap operas. She is the only African American to ever appear on *Leave It to Beaver* and the first black actress to appear on *General Hospital*.

Her numerous theater credits include the London premiere of Lorraine Hansberry's *A Raisin in the Sun*, *Desire Under the Elms*, *Like One in the Family* (NAACP Award and Drama-Logue Award Winner), and *Love Letters*, which she performed with her late husband, Werner Klemperer.

It is my hope in writing that Kim Hamilton, who is forever immortalized with Gregory Peck in the (uncredited) role of Helen Robinson during the climactic scene of *To Kill a Mockingbird*, will be honored, remembered, and recognized during this year's ceremony.

Thank you for your consideration.

CHAPTER 45

ELEANOR KEATON VISIT

I ARRIVED AT 11 A.M. for my meeting with Eleanor Keaton. She greeted me at the door, and we sat in the living room of her modest two-bedroom condo on a back street in Toluca Lake, California. Eleanor's friend Bart Williams, an actor, also joined us.

Eleanor told me that she had met Buster on the MGM lot when he was a gag writer and she was a dancer. Although she knew who he was, she had not been formally introduced until she expressed an interest in learning the game of bridge, a game at which Buster was a master. Eleanor was invited to sit in on bridge games off the lot and, over the course of the next year, saw Buster often but did not date him because he lived with someone else at the time.

When they both realized there was something more than friendship, Buster quietly set his living partner up with a bodybuilder from the lot, and Buster was, according to Eleanor, "dumped."

"The body-builder thing lasted three weeks," she told me. "Our relationship lasted twenty-one years."

It is clear to me that they were deeply in love. Eleanor said that she nurtured Buster in the later years of his life, keeping him active and engaged in the business, attending film screenings and encouraging him to perform. Buster had lost a significant amount of his hearing in service abroad during World War I, and although he regained it through medication early in life, as he aged, whenever a cold set in, he needed to go to the doctor for a treatment that would expand his collapsed eardrums. His inability to hear well affected his professional relationships with colleagues and directors, Eleanor said, but they performed together, and Eleanor was often there to guide the conversation along, especially in his final years.

We retraced much of Buster's film career in the three-plus hours we met. I talked through the story elements of the musical, and we discussed in depth Buster's relationships with Fatty Arbuckle, Joe Schenk, Natalie Talmage, and Charlie Chaplin, as well as his family vaudeville act. Eleanor referred to a trunk with memorabilia from the family that she said she would be happy to show me. We did not view this material during our visit, however.

As I had discussed with Eleanor on the phone, I told her that I have not fully developed my research for the structural elements of the show. At this time, a series of Busters serve as narrators; however, I have considered other alternatives since we have met. Eleanor talked about a few projects that were underway and offered the titles of several books on the subject for my review.

After a short overview, I offered to play the medley of eight songs I had prepared on cassette tape for the meeting. When I placed the tape into her cassette deck, it promptly jammed. The tape was not permanently damaged (I had a duplicate copy anyway), so I used the cassette recorder I had brought along to do the presentation.

After the medley, I presented Eleanor with a copy of the full proposal, and we worked through the story, stopping at the appropriate times to play the featured songs highlighted in the text. Eleanor was very engaged, stopping me at one point to note that the lyrics in the text were slightly different from those on the tape.

At the end of the presentation, Eleanor was complimentary. She felt strongly that a performance in the theater needed to tell a good story and leave you feeling refreshed, invigorated, and entertained. I listed a few shows, like *Crazy for You*, *Big River* and *The Will Rogers Follies*, as examples of the kind of energy I was reaching for in the music of the piece. Eleanor said that she had seen a production of *Beauty and the Beast* and always felt that the actor who played LeFou would be a great Buster in a show.

After the presentation, Eleanor and I went to lunch together at a local restaurant. Once there, we spoke more about personal moments and reflections in their lives together, as well as Buster's alcoholism and dismissal from MGM, which Eleanor felt needs to be told in the play; his divorce; and his fall from fame and the rejection that he felt at that time in his career.

Eleanor and Buster met late in his career: He was forty-five and she twenty-one, and he had been out of MGM as an actor for twelve years. Still, Eleanor felt that Buster lived a satisfying and full life, as his autobiography confirms, working actively in many areas of the business until his death in 1966.

We discussed the discovery of pristine prints of Buster's movies found on Buster's former estate, now owned by James Mason, in the early 1950s. The Keaton film archive—now part of the Rohauer Collection, which grew out of a 1954 business relationship with Raymond Rohauer—was stabilized on safety stock and became the basis for a resurgence of Keaton's popularity in movie houses, on television, in films, and at film festivals around the world.

Eleanor told me that although Buster never felt that these appearances were particularly important, one live appearance after a viewing of *The General* in Germany in the early 1960s led to a twenty-minute standing ovation.

After Buster's death in 1966, Eleanor sold the big house and moved into the condo. A few years ago, she purchased the other half of the building, anticipating that she would care for her ailing sister. Eleanor did not complete this story, so I assume that perhaps her sister may have passed away.

Eleanor attends Keaton film festivals and Keaton tributes around the country and in his hometown, where an annual festival is held honoring show business professionals. She is a personal friend of

Dom DeLuise (for whom I wrote the "I'm Fat and That's That" number in the show), who has a house in Dorset, Vermont. Eleanor said she would try to get the two of us together. (DeLuise is also a friend of the Sardis.)

Eleanor will turn eighty in a couple of months. She has arthritis in her back, which causes her discomfort when she sits or stands too long, but besides that and the advancement of age, to which she referred a few times in jest, she admitted that she is content in her life.

Eleanor offered to help in any way to make this project a success. She confirmed the relationship between the agent (Douris) and the estate, and she told me that she would be available to speak or meet with me further along as things progressed. She said that similar projects had stalled in the past, but since Gary Dartnell has purchased the rights to Buster's films, my project comes along at a good time.

I told Eleanor that my goal is to receive a letter of agreement from the agent to develop this project in the next six months to a year. I would then like to establish a creative team under the direction of a seasoned producer to bring the project forward. Eleanor told me as we parted that she felt this was a wonderful project and would give her support to it in any way she can.

NOVEMBER 20, 1997

Act II, Scene 3

Hands out, palms down
Press down
Press up
Palms up
Press up
Press down
Right hand, push out
Right hand, push in
Left hand, push out
Left hand, push in

Thompson:
Say "Ah!"

Joe:
"Aye"

Thompson:
No. "Ahhhh!"

Joe:
"Ah"

Dr. Thompson | Joe Gorilla
Act II, Scene 3

CHAPTER 46

ACT II, SCENE 3

SETTING: Dr. Thompson's Office

SONG: THE EXAMINATION

AT RISE: THOMPSON and NAN review the patient
             schedule and a new deficiency list, which
             is extensive.

THOMPSON has already seen five patients, and NAN
lists many more. There is a new patient as well.

THOMPSON asks NAN to bring that patient in now, and
he will move the others back.

NAN exits with door open as JOE and the CHAOSALS enter
THOMPSON's office. JOE is dressed as a carpenter,
and the CHAOSALS are his apprentices. All match in
bib overalls.

THOMPSON rises to greet the group. He asks if the
CHAOSALS are members of JOE's family. JOE says no,
that they are his crew, and that they are concerned

about this meeting today and wanted to be with him. THOMPSON tells them this is highly unusual, that he will perform an exam and delve into JOE's medical history. JOE suggests it might be better if they wait elsewhere. Perplexed and forlorn, the CHAOSALS exit.

NAN, JOE, and THOMPSON sing THE EXAMINATION. THOMPSON pokes and prods JOE GORILLA during the physical exam. The CHAOSALS appear when NAN opens and closes several different supply cabinets; however, only JOE can see them.

A nurse enters with results of the blood test and exits. JOE is anemic, low in vitamins C and D, has a calcium deficiency, has abnormally high cholesterol and triglycerides, has an irregular heartbeat, and is prediabetic, but otherwise shows no signs of serious illness.

THOMPSON suggests diet, exercise, and meds that could improve his numbers. JOE says he is on his feet all day and has no time to exercise, but he does enjoy volunteering for organizations and hopes that he might find some additional work in the center. THOMPSON tells him they are cutting back, that the center will close, and that they are only performing minimum maintenance right now, which is not enough.

JOE suggests that he spend the rest of the day in the center to determine if he and his crew can lend a hand. They could report back by the end of the day. THOMPSON thinks it is an interesting idea but needs the CHIEF's approval.

THOMPSON gives JOE a note with the deficiency list for the CHIEF. JOE says he'll take care of the CHIEF and exits.

BLACKOUT

CHAPTER 47

ACCOMMODATING CHEMOTHERAPY

Post Treatment

THREE WEEKS HAVE PASSED since my final chemotherapy treatment. Denise and I were married on New Year's Eve. We have taken a short honeymoon to Hawaii. I caught a twenty-two-inch, five-pound bonefish. Neither of us got tans. And now, we have returned to a somewhat normal schedule without an interruption every two weeks.

I misplace things much less often than before. My sense of humor is returning, and I am playing piano more, despite the neuropathy that will, no doubt, persist for some time. I have countered that with a speech-recognition program that has made writing easier. A few weeks ago, on an unusually warm Saturday in February, I took a nine-mile bike ride. It was glorious!

Throughout the months of December and January, I correctly anticipated that my treatments would become cumulative. We also hosted a wedding, took some pre-planned travel to New York City, and tried to enjoy the holidays, all of which proved to be especially challenging under the circumstances.

To accommodate the wedding plans, I moved my treatments from Monday to Friday. Previously, the most debilitating days of treatment period would fall on weekends. This change made those days fall in the middle of the week. Because of our production schedule, I had to anticipate when those days would occur and be sure that I was able to plan around them. It worked out, thanks to an accommodating staff, but wrapping up the treatment proved to be daunting.

The wedding was spectacular, all thanks to Denise, who planned everything. We included only members of our families and close friends with the promise that we would include everyone in a later event. We were able to plan to be away from a treatment schedule during that time. As a result, my energy was high, and, with our family and friends present, it was perfect for both of us.

FEBRUARY 2009

CHAPTER 48

KENNETH G. ALLEN NU '22—PERHAPS THE GREATEST TEAM EVER

COL Kenneth G. Allen USAR (Ret.), noted New York financial planner and lifelong friend of General I. D. White, Irving Berlin, Johnny Mercer and others on Tin Pan Alley, died January 13, 1992, in Northfield, Vermont. The following is an account of his college days playing on the Norwich polo team that participated in what the New York Times *reported was "probably the best game of indoor collegiate polo ever played."*

THE DATE IS MARCH 17, 1922. The arena, the Squadron A Armory, New York City. A trio from Norwich University, the oldest private military college in the country, sets its sights for the first round on the powerhouse in polo, Yale, at the intercollegiate polo championship. Who would have thought that the son of an Attleboro movie-house owner would team with a farmer's son from Newport, Vermont, and a future four-star in what The New York Times reported the following day was "probably the best game of indoor collegiate polo ever played"?

The early twenties evoke an image of a romantic time—after "the War to End All Wars" and before the Depression—when men in uniform and gentlemen on horses displayed class and dignity. The Norwich squad had crisscrossed the Northeast in 1921, posting impressive victories over Harvard, Army, Cornell and Penn. At home in Northfield, Vermont, on February 11, 1922—in perhaps its most triumphant victory over Princeton, 11 1–2 to 8—the team established itself as one of the best around.

It was not always that way. As any rider will tell you, it is the mark of a true horseman to have command of the animal on a polo field. Coupled with the quality of the horses available through the Army, the Norwich cadets struggled to gain the knowledge and ability to compete on the national level.

The polo program had been discontinued nine years before at the university. The team played private clubs, including the Brooklyn Riding and Driving Club, 101st Cavalry of Newark, the Springfield Riding and Driving Club, and various National Guard teams. Regardless of the score, the opponents left knowing that the horsemen from Norwich showed promise.

These were not ordinary men who traveled the country by train to compete from mid-November through March. They had names like Kenny "KG" Allen, James W. "Snow" Joslyn, and Dave "ID" White. Together with first-substitute Reggie Switzer, they had a purpose and a drive to succeed that carried them throughout their lives. Fate would play its hand, as well, in bringing these men together.

A young cadet of excellent ability, Ken Allen worked the hardest to master his talents. Early in the program, a room-sized cage of chicken wire and boards was erected above the riding hall. A sawhorse with saddle stood high in the center, with sloped boards settling down to the base. At every opportunity, indeed every night for hours, KG could be found smashing balls from atop the stationary horse. With each swing, his eyes and hands were matched with a grace and power that would become his trademark on the field as Number 1.

Snow Joslyn, the farmer's son, was easily the best rider of the crew. Snow spent years caring for the animals and riding through every conceivable situation. And once the polo mallet was placed in his hand, it became one with his body and the beast. Snow was the charger, the aggressor who never let up on the ball or the man.

Number 2.

The captain—and arguably the best collegiate horseman of his time—was Dave White. He was simply graceful, strikingly handsome, modest and forever a soldier. It was clear that White would be a leader of men from his first days on campus. And his talents with a horse are legendary; as a back in polo, unquestionably the best.

Early in the season of 1921, the team's Number 1 took a serious fall and withdrew. The coach, Colonel F. B. Edwards, had to replace him quickly and went to Dave and Snow for their suggestions. It was agreed that Ken Allen had the technical skills and the work ethic to be outstanding. But he was not an aggressive player in practice chukkers.

Dave White took Ken aside and told him that, in that day's heat, he must aggressively attack the practice squad to make an impression. At one stretch, Ken ran Colonel Edwards three times hard in the rail, which left no doubt that his selection as Number 1 would be assured. The horsemen now had all three qualities for success—Allen's flawless technique, Joslyn's competitive skill, and White's grace and style.

The friendship grew among these three over the following year, as did their reputation. Often spectators would stand in awe of the mastery the young cadets took to each heat. Some found themselves dumbfounded by the teammates' ability to outguess their opponents on the field.

There was a system.

It was simple and foolproof.

One night, the group decided they needed some signals on the field. They would give verbal commands to each other that should be ignored if they called each other "Ben." Ken would ride hard to the ball, and Dave would yell, "Hit it, Ben!" And as the opposing man would bear his animal on, Ken would ride hard toward and then over the ball, taking his man out. This would leave an easy shot for Dave, who took full advantage. And so did each member, as the games and legend grew.

At the Squadron A in March of 1922, the horsemen had just come off a grueling series of contests that took their toll. The Cleveland Tourney was followed by club matches to prepare for the finals. At the end of regulation, the score stood tied at 3–3. A wild overtime ensued. Yale showed skill and savvy that put the horsemen from Norwich to the test. An early flurry in the overtime put Yale up by one, and as time was running out, the Yale squad smashed another shot high in. The horsemen challenged and rode to bring it even, but time was up. Yale 5. Norwich 3.

Memories often fade on the once romantic time when men and horses played their games. KG and Dave called each other "Ben" throughout their lives. Dave became General I. D. White, Norwich's first four-star general and war hero. In his thirty-eight-year career on active duty, he commanded "Hell on Wheels," the famous 2nd Armored Division, through North Africa, Italy and Germany during WWII; served two tours in Korea; and was commander in chief of the US Army, Pacific. Snow Joslyn worked for the Sandy Hill Corporation for forty-two years, serving, finally, as first vice president and director. Both have passed away in recent years—Snow in 1984 and ID in 1990.

And KG rose to the rank of Army Reserve colonel Kenneth G. Allen. He was a noted annuities specialist and administrator in New York for more than sixty years, with lifelong associations with Irving Berlin, Johnny Mercer and others on Tin Pan Alley, and until recently, could be found at the Oyster Bar for lunch most every day, and at the Princeton Club on weekends.

A fall on November 9, 1991, forced the colonel to retire, at the age of ninety-one, from the company that bore his name, and seek rest and comfort in a familiar environment: a small town in the center of Vermont where men and horses long ago displayed grace and dignity. He passed away a few weeks after making it home to the hills of Vermont, a few hundred yards from where the horses once ran.

If you thought you heard the thunder of hooves recently, you know now that on January 13, 1992, the Horsemen were finally reunited in spirit.

And what a sight it was.

JANUARY 24, 1992

On Saturday, October 8, 1994, as part of the 175th anniversary celebration of Norwich University, members of the Sugarbush Polo Club held an exhibition match on the Norwich campus for the first time in more than forty-six years. The club recreated a 1922 match in which Norwich beat Princeton in Northfield. History repeated itself, as Norwich was again victorious by a score of 12 to 9.

CHAPTER 49

PEOPLE I KNEW— WALTER D. EHLERS, MEDAL OF HONOR RECIPIENT

Dear Catherine,

It was so sad to speak to you and learn of Walt's passing. For all the wonderful times we met to record interviews and the numerous visits along the way over the last seven years, I considered it a privilege to spend even a minute with him. Each time, I wanted to be sure that he knew how much respect I have for his service, his personal sacrifice, and for so generously sharing himself with everyone. Walt was an amazing human being.

The road he has traveled would challenge someone half his age, but for Walt to endure the medical treatments he needed to survive and still travel to talk to students, veterans, and service members, and represent the finest values of our country so completely, is a testament to his personal strength and will. I will always feel that each of the occasions that he came to Chicago or we met in New Orleans, California, or New York City, his participation was the rarest of gifts. I remember each of them so vividly, and with the help of video, I can share those experiences forever.

There have been several times over the last few months that I thought I would be writing a letter to you like this. I imagined that I would recall in detail the extraordinary events that surrounded his numerous combat landings, the medal action, the emotional moments he recalled about returning to Normandy years later, or the anguish he felt whenever he recalled his relationship with Roland.

The fact is, each time we got together, your dad taught me a little more about important things: life, survival, facing insurmountable odds, and the emotional healing process that only time provides. He had a wonderfully warm smile and a distinctive chuckle as he calmly recalled a fascinating moment in his life as if it happened yesterday. I sensed that each time we talked, he allowed me to walk along with him, experience the hollow feelings of loss—the human cost of war— and then made those moments bearable and survivable, perhaps a little easier for both of us to bear.

My thoughts of Walt this week have come to rest on several unforgettable moments during the 2009 Chicago Medal of Honor Convention. On September 17, at Wrigley Field after the field ceremony honoring the recipients, we passed out game jerseys with the recipient name and year of action on the back. *EHLERS 44.* A great combination!

I was also given a game baseball that day. Back on the recipient bus, I asked Walt to sign and date it. You and I mulled over whether to have other recipients do the same. In the end, I decided not to impose on everyone.

Two days later, we gathered fifty-two Medal of Honor recipients on the stage together for the opening of the Patriot Gala. It was the largest gathering of recipients on one stage in recent memory—a fitting tribute to those in attendance, but a number that Walt has seen decline steadily over his seven decades as a recipient. We took great care in making sure that each recipient could be seen by the audience and presented him respectfully. The look in the eyes of every recipient that evening will stay with me forever.

The lasting image I have of your dad is the extraordinary picture taken later that evening of the two of us, side by side. Two years later, during his last visit to the library with you, Walt signed that picture.

Throughout my association with the Medal of Honor Society, co-chairing the 2009 Chicago Annual Convention, and building the Pritzker's Medal of Honor archive of more than forty-seven live interviews with these extraordinary heroes, it has been a high honor and privilege to be in the same room with every one of our nation's most decorated combat veterans.

Cathy, you and your family have worked tirelessly to bring us along on your dad's journey. You will always have a special place in my heart for having such confidence in our work, for supporting your father's legacy, and for so lovingly making it possible to tell his story to the next generation.

Thanks for all this, and for my favorite photograph and Walt's baseball—both constant reminders of one of the most extraordinary men I have ever known. My thoughts and prayers have been with Walt and are with you, Dorothy and your entire family, now and always.

MARCH 3, 2014

• WALTER DAVID EHLERS •
May 7, 1921—February 20, 2014

CHAPTER 50

PEOPLE I KNEW— THOMAS J. HUDNER JR., MEDAL OF HONOR RECIPIENT

TOM HUDNER RECEIVED THE Medal of Honor for his actions after an attempt to save the life of his wingman, Jesse Brown, who had crash-landed his plane on a desolate mountaintop in the Chosin Reservoir area on December 4, 1950, during the Korean War.

Brown was the Navy's first Black aviator and the first Black American naval officer to lose his life in combat.

The following is a transcript of an interview taped in Denver in September 2007 with Hudner about his reflections on the action and serving with Brown.

As an introduction, I have included a brief narrative overview of our last telephone conversation in March 2014.

A truly remarkable man.

TOM HUDNER

On March 29, 2014, I called and spoke to Tom Hudner. It was not a formal interview as we'd had many of those in years past. He was, as always, soft-spoken, upbeat, and engaging. Among the topics we discussed was the Medal of Honor Society–sponsored Leadership Development Program, which has been expanding to schools across the country. Tom was particularly proud of the initiative, which brings recipients of the Medal of Honor into schools through personal visits and internet programs.

Hudner, a Korean War veteran, was the first recipient, by date, to receive the Medal of Honor after World War II. He remembers that at an early inauguration, a duty officer allowed him only one ticket because his guest was not his wife. He said that happened only once, and thereafter all recipients were invited to the presidential inauguration, but they had to pay their own way. (The number of living recipients then was perhaps five times greater than the current number of seventy-six living recipients.)

According to Tom, times have changed significantly. The recipients have been treated with extraordinary respect as they move from city to city for their annual conventions. The last major convention in Chicago was held in 2009 and attended by more than fifty heroes.

Tom talked about serving on the policy development committees in the early days of the Medal of Honor Society, which was formed in 1958. He has high regard for recent recipients like Sal Giunta, whom he has had a kinship with since meeting him, as well as the oldest recipients he met early in his life who had fought in World War I.

2007 CONVERSATION with Medal of Honor Recipient Tom Hudner—Denver, Colorado September 10, 2007
(This transcript has been edited for length and clarity.)

TOM HUDNER ON JESSE BROWN FIRST IMPRESSIONS

Ed Tracy: Tell me about your first impressions of Jesse Brown when you met. Describe who he was, the struggles he faced, and the challenges he overcame.

Tom Hudner: I got my wings in August of 1949, and my first orders were to the Naval Air Station on Long Island. Shortly after I got there, the squadron I joined was decommissioned, and I went to another squadron at the same station. It was only when I got my orders to this other squadron did I even hear of Jesse Brown. He had gotten his wings a year before I did, but I didn't know that there were any Black naval aviators. When I arrived in the squadron, nothing was said even at that time that Jesse was in the squadron. So, it was a day or two after I got there, when I was in the locker room getting ready for a flight, when Jesse came in. I wasn't startled, but I was a little bit surprised. He was very quiet. He just introduced himself. "I'm Jesse Brown." Very low-key. We had a few words that I really don't remember, and then I went out to the flight.

Of course, as in squadron life, we'd see each other on a daily basis. It was obvious from the very beginning that he was very well liked by everybody, but there was no deference in any way. He was just one of the guys. No thought whatsoever [about him being] Black.

ET: How would you describe him?

TH: Well, as I remember, he was probably about five ten or five eleven. Slender fellow. He was a track man, so he looked like a sprinter. With a ready smile. He had a great sense of humor. He was the butt of a lot of jokes, and he joked about a lot of other people, too. I wouldn't say that he was anybody special in the squadron except that not everybody was proud of the fact that he was there. Frankly, what made it better was he was a helluva good guy.

He was an ensign. He'd been an ensign for . . . I don't think he'd been an ensign for a full year, so he was one of the lowest-seniority guys in the squadron. He was given the responsibilities of a young officer in his position, as the Navy emphasized, you did small jobs to increasing responsibility as time and rank goes on. He didn't get his work done on a number of times, no more than anybody else, so the squadron CO would have to kick his butt to get his paperwork done and things like that. But he didn't experience anything that the rest of us didn't experience.

DATING AND MARRIAGE

TH: How long he was dating his future wife, Daisy, I don't know, but apparently they had been dating quite a bit. So, when he got into the flight program, he got in as a non-officer, and the Navy would not take married non-officers. As an officer, you could go through the program married. But as a non-officer, you couldn't.

He ran into the typical problems that Blacks faced at the time. Being down there in the South, especially Pensacola, no matter where he turned, he was given a hard time by people. The fact that he was a Naval aviation cadet didn't deter a lot of these people from saying anything. He experienced harassment a number of times while in uniform by shore patrol and others.

The flight program was demanding. He started in 1947, got his wings in 1948. There was a lot of pressure on students at that time.

I don't think his girlfriend, who came from Hattiesburg, could afford to come and see him at all. Whenever he had leave and did have a chance, he drove back from Pensacola to Hattiesburg to see her. I don't know how long a drive that would be, but not too much effort.

He was under so much pressure. He finally married Daisy while he was in the training program, which was very definitely against regulations. But she, of course, gave him much comfort and solace. I'm sure that he attributed being with her as an anchor.

Jesse and I were not very close. He was an ensign and I was a [lieutenant (junior grade)]. At that time, there was a big difference between an ensign and everybody else. He had very good friends who were my rank and were true friends. The difference, though considered minor, was a big one at the time.

Also, I was Naval Academy and had several Naval Academy friends before coming in there, and these other fellows, they were our friends too, but I gravitated toward those I knew before. So, that is why I didn't see Jesse more than I did. Plus, the fact that I was a bachelor and a couple of these friends were bachelors, too. We just didn't mix at all.

ON THE MOUNTAIN

ET: Take us through Jesse's crash and what you saw from above.

TH: In those days, for all takeoffs and landings, your canopy was open. The canopy would slide back and forth on rails. When it was open, there was a little latch that would flip over onto the track. So, if you made a sudden stop, it would keep the canopy from going forward.

When he landed and the canopy was open, I presumed he had latched it open. It latches open automatically. But he hit with such force that the canopy shut. So, we couldn't see him in the cockpit. As soon as this happened, the flight commander left us to climb to a higher altitude, because this is a mountainous terrain . . . and to call for assistance, presumably from the Marines because they were known to have helicopters in the area. So, several of us . . . three or four aircraft from other flights came over for curiosity or however they could help.

Then someone said, "He's waving at us." Jesse had managed to open the canopy . . . and we could see him. He was waving at us to let us know that he was alive. The flight commander came back on our frequency and said that helicopters were on the way. I don't know when it was said, but it would be as long as a half an hour before they could be there. In the meantime, smoke was coming out of the cowling back along the fuselage. That's when I thought, *By the time he gets here, the smoke could turn into flames.*

Our flight leader was still not on our channel, so I don't think I even called for permission to go in. When the time came, I just said, "I'm going in."

ET: He wouldn't have given you permission to go in anyway.

TH: No.

ET: Was there any buzz on the radio after you made the decision to go in?

TH: I don't remember any comments on the radio. There may have been some, but I don't remember any. It was not at all negative on the frequency. I don't know how many were on at the time, but no one said, "Don't do it." So, I've always said, "No one told me not to."

AT THE CRASH SITE

ET: So Jesse is out of his gloves and parachute. He has been trying to get out of the cockpit on his own. His hands are frozen. What are the conditions?

TH: There is about twenty inches of snow on the ground. Not constant, but it was knee-high. The weather was clear. I don't remember there being much wind at all, but it was cold.

I had a blue knit cap that sailors wear. They call them watch caps. I used to carry one of those in my flight suit in case I got stuck. He had taken his helmet off, and that was on the floor of the cockpit. So, I pulled the watch cap over his head, and I had a white Navy scarf and wrapped that around his hands, but it didn't do much good since his hands were so frozen.

The fire subsided. Hydraulic fluid or possibly oil dripped on the hot pipes and plumbing that went up through into that part of the airplane. It diminished as time went on. There was almost no wind, but what wind there was was blowing the smoke back up the fuselage, but not into the cockpit. I was waiting for the helicopter. Frankly, for lack of anything better to do, I was throwing snow on the fuselage, under the cowling, which did almost no good.

ET: Do you recall Jesse saying anything about Daisy at this time?

TH: One of the few things he said to me . . . he just said, "If anything happens to me, just tell Daisy how much I love her." There was no time for small talk, so we didn't talk.

ET: How soon did the helicopter come?

TH: It was about a half an hour. The helicopter pilot got the word that there was a plane down. The helicopter was a Sikorsky H03. There are pictures of them—one of the smallest. Not a bubble canopy, but spheroid, a lot of glass or plastic in the front of it. Maximum capacity was three: pilot, copilot, and crewman. The pilot took off with a crewman to help get Jesse out of the cockpit. When he heard afterward that there were two of us on the ground, he had to turn around and go back and let the crewmen off. He was going in there all by himself. He didn't know what the circumstances were. The planes went down is about all he knew.

ET: So, that trip back took even more time for him to get there.

TH: Oh yes. That had to add at least fifteen minutes to it. I don't know if I told you this, but when we left Norfolk, Virginia, on the way over to Korea, the day we got underway, we went up on deck, there are six helicopters there with a Marine detachment, so there were ten pilots and supportive enlisted personnel. We took them all to Korea from there, which was the better part of two weeks. We left the first of September and didn't have our first flight until the tenth of October.

These Marines were riders. They didn't fly well, and when you go through several time zones, no one can sleep. We still had our work to do, but these guys didn't . . . what I'm leading up to is that, after being on the ship for the better part of a month, the rescue pilot came and saw the only Black face in naval aviation in the cockpit. I don't recall if he said anything to Jesse. Jesse was comatose at the time. In and out of consciousness. He was very calm, but we think that he was in shock. I sometimes wonder how he could have been talking at all.

ET: Was he saying anything that made sense?

TH: I don't remember that he did. There was so little conversation between the two of us. I didn't spend much time in the cockpit. It was difficult. Very hard to get up there. I went back to my plane to give a status report. My radio was still working. Some said I shouldn't have turned it off, but I conserved the batteries so the radio would work longer.

ET: Were there enemy patrols in the area?

TH: I am told by some who were flying in the area that there were, but they were not close, and I saw no evidence except a single set of footprints . . . tracks in the snow. Getting up a couple of times to check on Jesse is all that I did. I was just trying to encourage him to stay long enough to help Jesse. Jesse said virtually nothing while Charlie and I were trying to figure out what to do, [while] in the back of our minds, I think, knowing there is nothing we can do.

ET: Once the axe comes out . . . you can't chop steel with an axe.

TH: Charlie was naïve just asking for an axe.

ET: So, at one point Charlie looks at you and says, "Tom, it's getting dark."

TH: Charlie turns to me and says, "Tom, it's getting dark and I can't fly . . . I don't have the instruments to fly at night. I'm going. It's up to you what you want to do, but I've got to get outta here." It wasn't a matter of being chicken or anything. It was just the reality. Frankly, Jesse may have been dead at the time he said it. I said, "We don't have the equipment to get you out of here. We're going back to get something." I don't know . . . he didn't say anything, but I don't know if he even heard what I said to him. My only hope is that, looking back on it, that he knew he wasn't alone at the time he passed. No matter what the circumstances, we don't want to be alone at that time.

ET: I know how difficult this is to bring back. I cannot tell you how much I appreciate the time you've spent today talking about this.

TH: Jesse got his wings just about the time that President Truman issued the executive order to desegregate the armed services. The Navy had the reputation of being the most segregated due to the particular nature of the Navy. The posts aboard ship. Not being able to get away. He came into the Navy on active duty as an officer into a recently desegregated Navy. Just because of the proclamation, the executive order, didn't mean that anybody felt any differently about it. It isn't that he ran around the ship and said, "Because of this executive order, you have to treat me differently." He wasn't that way at all.

Jesse was somebody that showed right from the day we met his reticence to force himself . . . or break anybody's personal zone. He didn't even offer to shake hands at first. He didn't want anybody to say that they didn't want to shake hands with him. He was very respectful. He didn't have any attitude, haughtiness, subservience. He was just one of the guys. Just from his attitude again, everybody did truly like him.

I ran into people years later who were in the squadron before I got there who spoke very admiringly of Jesse. It was pretty obvious that, if he had stayed in the Navy, which I do not believe were his intentions, he'd have been a leader. Whether he would have been the first Black admiral, I don't know.

He was a decent person. He could have been a son of a bitch to the stewards and the others, but he wasn't. The stewards hovered around him, which is a very natural reaction. I don't think he went out of his way . . . never got friendly with enlisted personnel. He was an officer.

Although Jesse was only an ensign, because of his breaking through this big, big barrier to become a Navy aviator, he was really a role model. Everyone respected him, and he was certainly headed for better things. He was accepted at Ohio State University. After he served his time, his intentions were to become an engineer or maybe even an architect. Whatever he'd have done, he would have been fine.

ET: When you returned, what was the mood back on the ship knowing that Jesse was gone?

TH: There was a big void. He wasn't just one of the guys who happened to fit in. He's the type of guy, not to dramatize it, but lights would shine when Jesse came in. He was not a back-slapper either. He'd come in unobtrusively. He'd play acey-deucey with a lot of the guys. He was well liked.

Before we deployed, he had a hard time as a new naval aviator with a new wife. He couldn't find any housing. I'm guessing that he looked up to fifteen miles away for a house or room to rent, and everyone said, "Just missed it" or "Too late." There was a Black enlisted man pay officer who somewhat befriended him. He found a place for him near Providence. So, it was not just a few miles off the base. He had to go that far up, in the nonsegregated New England. Think about what it would have been anywhere in the South.

But he was philosophical about it. A lot of the new squadron mates were helpful to him, but there was a limit to what they could do, too.

I was always a little disappointed that the Navy didn't make more of Jesse Brown. There was such an emphasis on bringing Blacks in. If Jesse had been just an ordinary guy who got caught in something . . . but he was a guy at a very low level, rank-wise, who was an inspiration, not only to the other Blacks, but everyone who knew about him. But they didn't do more about it.

Throughout my career, I always heard about the Tuskegee Airmen, but I learned that there was more than one Tuskegee Airman, and Jesse was just one guy. As I met some of them, they had never heard of Jesse Brown.

I think the word is getting around. Part of the heritage of the naval aviators is the story of Jesse Brown.

• THOMAS JEROME HUDNER JR. •
August 31, 1924—November 13, 2017

Act II, Scene 4

Busy, busy all day long
Busy busy. Always on.

The Chaosals
Act II, Scene 4

CHAPTER 51

ACT II, SCENE 4

SETTING: Treatment Room

SONG: BUSY BUSY, VERY BUSY

ON RISE: It is a busy day in the treatment room. The shift changes and the IMPATIENT PATIENT, who has to wait, refuses to cooperate.

The CHAOSALS appear stuffed in closets and behind doors but are otherwise unseen by those onstage as they move patients in and out while singing and dancing to BUSY BUSY, VERY BUSY.

At the conclusion of the number, the scene transitions to the Chief's Office.

CHAPTER 52

NEW QUARTERBACK

January 29, 2010

Dr. Jack Morgan
Dr. Robert Lane
Dr. Richard Freeman
Dr. Arthur Bowles
Dr. Edith Lloyd

I am writing you to request a review of my medical status and to ask for your opinion about the proper course of action for the future.

This weekend marks the one-year anniversary of the completion of my six-month, twelve-session chemotherapy regimen following my colorectal surgery on July 17, 2008, for stage 3C colon cancer. I have been under the excellent care and observation of my surgeon and friend, Dr. Jack Morgan, and my oncologist, Dr. Robert Lane, since my surgery, with routine visits to Dr. Arthur Bowles.

I was advised this week by Dr. Lane that my oncology review would now be on a four-month cycle. My second colonoscopy was completed last summer. I will not have to return until 2012. All tests have been excellent. This is very good news.

Surgery and chemotherapy treatment aside, the lingering effects of chemo and the neuropathy that I deal with has been the main focus over the past year—particularly over the past five months, when the condition worsened to include severe muscle pain, leg pain, and depression. In December 2009, a blood test disclosed that I had abnormally low cholesterol (109). Dr. Lane reduced my dosage of Lipitor from 80 mg to 10 mg. The constant muscle pain in my legs that I was experiencing has reduced significantly, but still exists.

In total, I have lost more than fifty pounds from my pre-surgical weight in July 2008—perhaps more. I have been particularly successful in the past six weeks, having lost ten pounds through a strict diet, and I now weigh 228 pounds. I do not drink alcohol because of the various medications I am taking. I also do not prefer to exercise in a gym, and never have, but I try to walk often. I have not had the opportunity over the past two summers to ride my bike as I did before the surgery, but I expect that this summer I will be able to do so. I'd like to get back on the golf course someday, having played most of my life, but not for the past several years.

During the last two months, I now realize that I became dependent on Norco to relieve neuropathy and leg pain. I have had a regular prescription of Norco for several years for chronic back pain. I have needed, since early on in chemotherapy, a significant dose of Lunesta to sleep. Over the past year, I have used Ambien to sleep each night. In response to the developing anxiety in early December, Dr. Lane prescribed Lexapro.

I have continued to work from Labor Day 2008, seven weeks after surgery, to date. I enjoy my work. It is challenging and rewarding, but also stressful. Despite all of the medical issues, I was productive through October 2009. Both Denise and I noticed a definite change in attitude and temperament in early November 2009 that I attribute to the overmedication of Lipitor and resulting effects over time. It may also be related to the fact that over the period of my recovery, I did not properly process all that had occurred.

I discontinued my use of Norco on Friday, January 22. While it was the only medical treatment that seemed to provide enough relief from the symptoms of the neuropathy to get on with life, my digestive system shut down early on Saturday, January 23. Thanks to Dr. Morgan for his patience and guidance through this difficult situation.

I am now completely off Norco and, at Dr. Lane's direction, trying Lyrica for the neuropathy—a treatment plan I tried for six weeks in July 2009. I have been meeting with Dr. Lloyd for three weeks to help me sort things out. I feel that I am in a better situation now than I have been in several months.

On Tuesday, I completed an EMG test and am scheduled to review the results with Dr. Freeman on February 8, my second appointment. I will continue to take Lyrica and look forward to Dr. Freeman's review of my test results in an effort to resolve the neuropathy.

At this juncture, a review of my medical condition and a new medical plan appears to be in order. I would like to propose that the best course for me is to schedule surgery to remove the port-o-cath, conduct a review, and develop a reasonable treatment plan through one physician. I will appreciate your advice and direction.

A great number of people have been responsible for my care over the last two years. Northwestern Hospital has provided superb professional treatment for me. I've been given a second chance to enjoy each day and have been single-minded in my attempt to understand what is happening and to make the best choices. I've rounded a corner emotionally in recent weeks and appreciate your help in advising me on the next course of medical treatment to keep moving forward.

Thank you for your time, your professional expertise, and for all that you have done to support Denise and me in this journey. We are very grateful for your kindness and attention.

PEOPLE I KNEW— ROBERT M. JOHNSON

Dear Pep,

It has taken me awhile to write this to you. Putting the first few words on paper, and looking back at them, I realize that I have not written nearly enough over the past few years. We communicate so differently now, through social media, on the phone, and by email, that I do not feel like we are out of touch, but writing is such a wonderful exercise, and it is something that is much more permanent than any of the other alternatives.

I have been conflicted about just what to say as well. I wanted to be sure that when I wrote, it was after I had time to reflect on all that you and Bob have done for me, often at times when I was on the ledge and had no one else to talk to. Everyone needs a "crisis brother," and since the day we met, Bob was mine. I never expected that you and Bob would become so important in my life, and to the lives of my family, particularly Amanda. Through your loving support and generosity, we have all learned how to be better family members, friends, and human beings.

I have tried to remember the exact moment in 1989 that I met Bob. Like a lot of alumni in the early days at Norwich, it was no doubt during my first homecoming weekend at a Partridge Society Board meeting and surely at the suggestion of another mentor, John Stone, who saw a kinship of spirits between Jason, Bob, and me and encouraged me to listen and learn from them.

During that time, I was busy getting established at Norwich, building the log cabin—which we did not complete until Christmas that year—and traveling the Northeast between Vermont and New York, trying to keep the NORWICH 2000 capital campaign on course. Bob and Jason were certainly engaged in that effort, and Bob was interested in the small-but-energetic alumni group we were forming in New York City. He felt, as I did, that New York was the next big region outside of Boston to make a significant impact.

In those days, Bob was referred to as the "Right Reverend Johnson" and would always be called upon to give the blessing at university functions. He was earnest, present in the moment, and had just the right amount of playful candor that made everyone feel good about the university and the people who were supporting us. A word of welcome from Bob Johnson was a terrific way to start any evening.

At the time, Norwich's campaign organization involved class leaders—which Bob and Jason were surely among—and it was a volunteer system. With so much campaign staff turnover, however, we were sorely in need of some excitement, momentum, and a fresh approach. NORWICH 2000 closed successfully, and a series of events to celebrate Norwich's 175th anniversary provided an opportunity for the alumni all over the nation to hear directly from MG Todd.

In the years that followed, things started to evolve. President Schneider completed the 175th anniversary celebration in 1994 with a huge event honoring Medal of Honor recipient Captain James Burt, which included W. E. B. Griffin, the successful writer that Bob was integral in keeping in the Norwich family and who helped found the Colby Symposium with the late Ambassador William Colby and Carlo D'Este. I will not elaborate on Bob's passion for and overall contribution to the Colby except to say that it was immediate, unrelenting, and vitally important to those early days. I will state for the record that it is hard to imagine any scenario that involves the Colby Symposium becoming a reality without the support of Bob Johnson and the committed group of alumni and friends that he and Jason gathered together. They were the lifeblood of the program.

The same could be said for every initiative that Bob got involved with at Norwich. He was instrumental in the expansion of membership in the Partridge Society. I vividly recall driving from Vermont to Boston to meet Bob with hundreds of letters for him to sign for members and potential donors to help the cause. We sat in the lobby bar of his hotel, and Bob carefully wrote a personal note on every letter. Bob was the catalyst—a personable guy with a genuine quality to make anyone feel welcome and at home.

Bob was the first person outside New York City to support the "Norwich Nights on Broadway" program that helped to rally alumni support for the symposium and helped to bring new friends into the Norwich family. Those weekends in New York, and in Washington at the National Press Club, were some of the most exciting high-end events ever for Norwich alumni, with the likes of Sally Shelton, Phil Caputo, Rick Atkinson, and Stansfield Turner. Norwich's reputation was growing because of the consistent support of leaders like Bob.

It's great to look back at the happy times, particularly those trips to New York when Bob accommodated a large group, and we were in the room with Vincent Sardi, Werner Klemperer (Colonel Klink), Joyce Randolph (*Honeymooners*), Bernadette Peters, cast members from *Titanic*, and the big moment when Robert Goulet dropped into the reception and made everyone's day. (I personally did not see what all the fuss was about, but the women in the room swooned!)

I was also taken to task a few times, like when I invited Bob and a small group to the log cabin and made an inappropriate comment about "my" decision not to install a dishwasher. As I recall the most insensitive moment—truly a low point—of my life, Bob asked me where the dishwasher was going to be, and I moved to the sink and said, "Mary will stand right here." I don't think I ever saw him as angry and disappointed in me as in the next ten minutes. I apologized to Mary—and never said anything like that even jokingly again—and promised Bob that I'd order a dishwasher the next day. The happy ending is that the dishwasher arrived three days later.

There were many more serious times in our relationship when you and Bob comforted me, as when both of my parents passed in that first year, and following my divorce when you and Bob made the condo in Gulf Shores available. I spent three days at the Flora-Bama Bar and don't regret a minute of it, but never did anything like that again. And more than a few times, I called Bob to tell him that the best days of Norwich were behind me and that I was going to walk away. I never did, but if it had not been for Bob, I would have made a string of bad decisions on my own.

It's hard to quantify Bob's impact on the future of Norwich, but the most memorable example, for me, was his leadership and participation in 1996 at a small engineering charrette on campus about the future of the Engineering, Math and Science Building project during the Leadership Campaign. The university's facilities office proposed a plan to restore and upgrade the existing math and science hall that was adjacent to the library, versus an earlier proposal to build a new building, which had been determined to be cost prohibitive. The group took the bold position that the campaign leadership should expand their financial goals to include a completely new facility—the EMS Center that is the most prominent academic facility on campus today. Bob was instrumental in that decision and, soon after, proposed and provided design and fabrication services for the air system for the center—an extraordinary, and somewhat unheralded, leadership gift to Norwich University. In a state that prides itself on its air quality, the air in the EMS Center is second to none.

Nothing speaks to Bob's human side more than his love for you, for his family and for his friends. I know that Bob was always someone I could turn to, and I was pleased to be included in helping plan family gatherings and social events with you, Jason, Mary Jo, and your other friends who were included. From the excitement of Broadway shows and dinner out in New York to the Meet the Authors dinner at the Colby Symposium and cigars on the back porch at the Northfield Inn with Tom Clancy, W. E. B. Griffin, Joe Galloway, Frank Sesno, or H. R. McMaster, it was always time well spent with the "Right Reverend Johnson."

I can tell you that there is no deeper regret I have than being told at the airport, after waiting hours on standby, that I could not get out of Chicago in time to attend services for Bob in Birmingham. I would have told you and your family many of these things in person if I had. It's a small consolation that I have been able to recall so many wonderful times in the past few days. I have so much respect and love for you and Bob and only want you to know how much I appreciate all the things you have done over the years to make me feel so special.

The kindness and support that Bob gave to me will always be a source of great comfort. I will miss him dearly.

FEBRUARY 28, 2020

• ROBERT M. JOHNSON •
October 22, 1938—February 5, 2020

CHAPTER 54

PEOPLE I KNEW—
EDWARD J. FEIDNER—
SIMPLE LESSONS

THERE ARE MANY SIMPLE lessons in life. And all of them can be learned in a theater.

The trick? To remember those lessons when we need them the most.

I owe my love of theater—and degree in life—to one man: Ed Feidner.

Ed Feidner appeared, with a sweeping stride, a book balanced on his head, posing inside the door as if he had just dismounted his noble steed in the courtyard. It was a quiet day in the green room of the Arena Theater in 1972. I was a freshman in the department, hard at work preparing a scene with my acting partner, Jody Jarvis.

"Jody," he said, "I am in need of a maid for our play. Will you do it?" Jody paused for only a moment—no one would consider denying a personal invitation from Ed Feidner to be in a show—and then she agreed.

Mission accomplished, Ed turned effortlessly toward the door, and, as he took the grand pageantry of his balancing act off into the distance, I said, in a high-pitched voice, "Need another maid?"

Ed stopped, turned slowly, and took three steps in our direction, eyes locked down through the bottommost portion of the glasses perched at the tip of his nose, the book still firmly balanced on his head.

"No," he said defiantly.

He paused, dramatically.

"But I could use an orderly."

In the lowest tone that I could muster, I said, "I'll do it."

"Have you ever carried a samovar?" he asked.

"Of course," I said, not knowing at all what it was.

"Great," he said. "Just great. Get one and be at the theater tonight at six." And with that, he turned, and, with a slight dip in his step to show that he was in complete control, left us to continue our work, confident that we were now both part of the next Ed Feidner extravaganza—Anton Chekhov's *Three Sisters*.

A samovar is a large urn, made heavier by the liquid it carries—traditionally hot water for tea—and must be held outstretched like a platter. My introduction to UVM theater was to stand tall with the samovar for what seemed like twenty minutes, arms taut, while everyone else on stage swirled all around, hither and yon, extolling Chekhov.

Lesson One: Ask for the sale.

Lesson Two: Know what you're selling before you ask for the sale.

Ed Feidner took risks. He produced or directed almost all of Shakespeare's plays, including a blue jean–clad Caesar with switchblades and at least two productions in which he played Lear. There was a musical version of the first American play, Royall Tyler's *The Contrast*; several world premieres, including the rock musical *Covenant*; and of course, during our era, *West Side Story*—a show I am convinced he selected because a number of us felt it was time for UVM theater to mature into the musical realm at all costs. We had one small problem: We had few singers; no dancers; and a good, but overcommitted, orchestra. And still through it all, Ed was convinced that we would be great! Just great!

Early in the rehearsal process, in which I was cast as Riff, Ed placed me on a tall stepladder high above the other Jets. It was a team-building exercise meant to encourage the gang to look up to me as their leader. All about respect. But Ed quickly noted that it would not be easy for any of us—that we would have to earn respect along the way. It was a hard concept for all of us at that age, and not part of the early-'70s let-it-all-hang-out culture.

He wanted them to trust me—and for me to trust them. So, he instructed me to take a few steps down the fourteen-foot ladder and fall backward into the sea of humanity below. I had never done this before, and at more than 160 pounds and rugged, I would be a challenge for them to catch.

But, of course, they did, and the Jets all bonded together. Each one would climb the ladder and take his turn to help build a special trust with each other that day.

Lesson Three: Respect, like trust, is earned.

Lesson Four: Falling backward off a stepladder does not make you a better dancer.

Through the years, I would often stop in to talk to Ed in his office in the Craftsbury Room at the Royall Tyler. He always had time to speak to me, and was interested in my opinion, although he would rarely agree with almost anything I had to say.

Ed was my academic adviser. I asked him if I could continue my acting studies in graduate school.

"Ed," he said, "some people should just go out, get a job, and go to work. All this academic stuff is just not for you."

He referred to my inability to study at any level. I was a horrible student with about-even odds of graduating from UVM at all.

Ed helped me along because he knew that I loved the business. I was there all the time in those days, listening and exploring, playing piano, volunteering for this show or that one. Eventually I received work-study positions, first in the scene shop with technical director Bill Schenk, and then in public relations in the front office. I wanted to know more about it all—how to direct, act, hang lights, build sets, do makeup, stage manage, and work the front of house and public relations. He saw all that passion in me but knew, instinctively, that my life would not be spent in an academic theater environment.

The faculty at UVM, led by Ed, Bill Schenk, George Bryan, and Nancy Haynes, and staffed by Barbara Phillips, let us all grow on our own. They gave us the tools to be successful—and even allowed us to fail from time to time to build our characters so we could see how glorious success is when you work hard for it. Through each growing experience, we became better students, team players, stronger adults, more self-assured, and better able to think and act on our feet in all kinds of situations.

In the last semester of my senior year at UVM, I failed the second course of my educational career: film appreciation. I had withdrawn, failing, from cultural anthropology the semester before—after missing the drop deadline by a day. I failed the film course because I missed an essential element in passing the course: I never watched the films.

The consequence of not passing either course meant that I would be three credits short of the total required to earn a bachelor's degree, so I would be unable to graduate in 1976 with my class. After I failed to get any help from my instructor to retake the final exam, I went to Ed Feidner for counseling. We mulled over the few courses of action available. I was panicking because I had made commitments outside Burlington and did not plan to return for a whole semester, particularly for three credits, in the fall.

At the time, UVM allowed students to test out in courses for $10 a credit hour. When I suggested this to Ed, he peered down at me from behind the small antique desk in his office and said, "Be serious. Is there any subject you know so well that you could test out?"

He was right.

It was a bad idea.

All I knew besides theater was sports.

Sports!

There were half-credit gym courses available, and I had been an all-around athlete in high school four years before. Ed did not think for a moment it was possible, but he did make a call to the head of the physical education department on my behalf—a call that would change my life.

It was a little like visiting the Wizard of Oz, except the head of the physical education department at the time was a woman whose name to this day I do not recall. After I pleaded my case, she said, "I'll agree to approve this rather extraordinary request if you find six different instructors to test you in six different sports."

So, off I went.

In the next three days, I took soccer and softball written exams, drove a pail of golf balls, played one-on-one and shot foul shots with the assistant basketball coach, swam laps and treaded water for a total of half an hour, and dined—and bowled—with the bowling coach, a woman named Marilyn, I believe. I passed each of the six exams, returned for my departmental approval, and ran to the Waterman building just two days before graduation with my check for $30 in hand.

All was right with the world.

At commencement, when my name was read and I crossed in front of the faculty seated onstage, I smiled at Ed Feidner, who beamed that wonderful grin from ear to ear. Was it pride in my accomplishment or perhaps satisfaction that another close call with a student had been averted?

As a postscript to this story, you cannot do what I did at UVM today. Incensed by the ability of any student to test out in credits to earn a degree, the instructor who failed me petitioned the College of Arts and Sciences. The faculty held a hearing. Both Ed Feidner and Bill Schenk attended. They believed that if a student had fulfilled all distribution and degree requirements, whatever manner the other credits were obtained within the rules should be sufficient to graduate.

So, UVM changed the rules.

But both Ed and Bill told me later that it was great fun to be part of it all, and they had one more wonderful story to tell future generations of students.

Lesson Five: If you want something badly enough, never give up.

Ed Feidner was the ringmaster, the cavalier, a silver-clad knight riding on his trusty steed. His mind worked faster and on a different wavelength from most people. Many of us felt that he had no idea what he was talking about most of the time. But deep behind those impassioned eyes, overdramatic delivery, and scholarly attitude, his creativity was erupting, and he would bring to life a printed word, or, perhaps his greatest lesson of all, find strength and power in the silence of a moment.

Once long ago, Ed told me that great works of art in the theater are cyclical in nature, meaning that they often end where they began. I believe that when all is said and done, my friend and mentor Ed Feidner walks across a dimly lit stage, toward a brilliantly streaming amber-colored spotlight, on the verge of giving one more great performance. There is a strong, deliberate look in his eye, but he does not speak. He plays the quiet time . . . waiting for just the right moment to begin.

I screened Kenneth Branagh's masterpiece *Hamlet* recently and thought about Ed Feidner during many scenes. I was mysteriously transported back to a class or a rehearsal or a cup of coffee in his office when he would tell me about the significance of the ghost, how its appearance might be magically staged—or where and with what lighting and costumes. I remembered long passages of Shakespeare that I memorized and recited for enjoyment, to pass the day, prepare for a class, or to just keep up with him when he went off on a tangent during our many talks.

Through the years at UVM, I always felt that, although I may have been failing as a scholar, Ed gave me high marks for being a creative person.

There are many simple lessons in life. And all of them can be learned in the theater.

The trick? To remember those lessons when we need them the most.
I owe my love of theater—and degree in life—to one man: Ed Feidner.

APRIL 25, 2008

• EDWARD J. FEIDNER •

February 26, 1931—April 24, 2008

CHAPTER 55

DEAR JOHN—OLD FRIENDS

Dear John,

I have been thinking a lot recently about old friends.

We have very few actual old friends. We have mostly older friends—those kind souls who entered our lives in their advancing years and filled a void left in our minds and hearts by others gone by.

You almost need some sort of system to quantify who an old friend is—a checklist of certain qualifications to be met or used as a guide along the way. But then again, who's counting? In the end, the person we call "old friend" is an old friend forever.

So in the absence of any other reference material, here's the result of a very unscientific evaluation about what it takes to be an old friend.

Longevity

No matter how old you are, an old friend needs to have known you for more than 30 percent of your life. You may have known people longer, but if you have had no direct or indirect contact with them in more than 30 percent of the time you have known them, they do not qualify. You can still refer to these people affectionately as "someone I went to high school with," "the kid who taught me to throw a curve ball," or "my first wife."

Shared Life Experiences

There almost always needs to be a huge number of shared life experiences before anyone can be considered a close old friend. Those events grow exponentially for old friends and run the gamut of good times and bad, joy and anger, quiet and loud.

Pride in Accomplishment

I think of old friends with a large amount of pride for who they have become, the families they have raised, their professional accomplishments and the choices they have made in their lives, as well as the ways I have been included or how I may have helped them sort through them, and vice versa. It's important for old friends to recognize each other's accomplishments in special ways.

Humility

Old friends get along better if their values align with each other. Otherwise, there will come a time that you will have to part ways on a particular topic or position. These can sometimes be long-lasting and even permanent separations—which ultimately leads to one of the true indicators of an old friend: whatever happens, you can both find common ground, accept that we are all human and will make poor choices and hurtful mistakes and forgive.

Telepathy

It will be an ongoing test with an old friend. One clear sign is stubbornness in the face of what you might feel is an inconsequential item. Even as conversation with others turns to this topic or that one, you already know how your old friend will reply. And just about when that happens, you look at each other and telepathically admit that neither of you should go there.

It's the Little Things

Between old friends, memories are so intertwined that they can't remember exactly who did what and why. Each may have a clear memory of the event, but they muddle the facts in such a way that the teller of the tale almost always provides a different version of the story, which the other friend denies and corrects ad nauseam, until both old friends give up and move on to some other topic.

Romance

Old friends rarely endure through matters of the heart—that is to say that if matters of someone's heart come between two old friends, ultimately a choice must be made. I have never been on one side of this axis, but I have been twice on the other. With the passage of three decades to reflect on those abrupt decisions, I think I can safely say, on both counts, that I'd rather have the old friendships right about now. I cannot speak to the feelings of those on the other side though, since those relationships, while intense, never cleared the longevity requirement.

Right about now, my dad would say, "No use cryin' over spilt milk." He said that a lot.

Honesty

Old friends never have a problem telling you what they think. Old friends will tell you an enormous amount about what you should do, even when you do not ask and especially if alcohol is involved. Most of these observations are brutally honest and can cause trouble in other parts of your life. The truth hurts and sometimes is so painful to talk about that you need an old friend who can handle it.

Synergy and Validation

And then, in the relative calm of your life, an old friend will reemerge. You face this reappearance with anticipation, and you open an emotional drawer of memories that had been closed or long forgotten: adventures relived; late-night stories of lost loves, joy, laughter, music, and great food; and a wide array of feelings that contributed to the people you have become. It is in these times that we may realize long-lost old friends have reappeared to remind us that they do exist, that all those stories we have been thinking about are real, and that, for a brief time, there is one other human being alive who can provide validation.

Surviving Change

And then the Joni Mitchell lyric that applies to paradise and people comes to mind: "Don't it always seem to go that you don't know what you've got 'til it's gone."

Sadly, many old friends come and go from our lives—some off to another life apart from ours that includes other interests, goals, and people with whom to share those new life experiences. Most go because it is the right thing for them to do—that makes their life better and happier.

Others choose to move on emotionally. The best of old friends never let you know that. They'll always be there one way or the other if you need them, but, in reality, they are not there all the time.

Still others leave this earth altogether—some so suddenly that you are left to ponder great questions about all they left behind. The sadness you feel for the loss of an old friend might be the biggest qualification of all. No matter how old you are or how long you have known a person, the sudden, tragic loss feels so final that it moves you on many different levels.

It seems that when the lofty phrase "old friend" is used, we're really saying that this person knows us better than anyone and vice versa—that they will always be on your side. Even when they might not agree with your ultimate intentions, they can understand your position, so long as it does not cross moral and ethical boundaries.

We have very few actual old friends. We have older friends—those kind souls who entered our lives in their advancing years and filled a void left in our minds and hearts by others gone by.

You almost need some sort of system to quantify who an old friend is—a checklist of certain qualifications to be met or used as a guide along the way.

But then again, who's counting? In the end, the person we call "old friend" is an old friend forever.

Forever is a long time, old friend.

JULY 23, 2012

Act II, Scene 5

Be on time
that's what my mother said.
Make him wait
that's what my mother said.
(there's a line here that I haven't
written yet but it will sure be great)
Double down, that's
what my mother said
to me.

Katharine
Act I, Scene 5
(First draft)

CHAPTER 56

ACT II, SCENE 5

TRANSITION: Katharine at center sings reprise.

SETTING: Chief's Office

SONG: WHAT MY MOTHER SAID (Reprise)

AT RISE: The CHIEF is working hard in his
                 office, his desk piled with reports
                 and briefing surveys. He looks
                 stressed and consumed.

The CHIEF hums BUSY BUSY, VERY BUSY as the door
opens and JOE enters unseen. The CHIEF senses a
presence, appears nervous, but ignores the feeling
and goes back to work.

He hears a knock on the door, and an assistant
enters with a stack of forms for signature. The
assistant exits and JOE begins circling again.

JOE looks over the CHIEF's shoulder and points out,
one by one, four items in front of him. With each

discovery, the CHIEF grows more excited and starts
making notes and signing documents.
JOE places a paper on the top of the pile and the
CHIEF unwittingly signs it. With the paper in hand,
JOE exits, and the CHIEF calls CHUCK, the board
chair, about his new great idea.

FADE OUT AND TRAVEL MUSIC TO WAITING ROOM

CHAPTER 57

HAPPY TO SEE ME . . . GO!

IN THE DAYS THAT followed our wedding, I went to the hospital for my tenth treatment with my daughter, Amanda. It was a chance for her to see what I had been talking about. Amanda has spent an amazing amount of time in hospitals in recent years with my granddaughter, who was born prematurely. Amanda works for the March of Dimes in the NICU unit of a hospital. The two of us now would understand more about my condition.

It is hard to explain these kinds of things to family members unless they actually see them firsthand or they are already a member of "the Club." I've been fortunate in my life that our family has been supportive of each other in times of need. I wouldn't want it any other way.

In the chemo ward, I realize that this is a challenge for patients on many different levels. So it was with some expectation, high anticipation, but no cheer, that I approached my final treatment on January 30.

I received a phone call at the time from an associate. Having heard of my condition, my friend wanted to let me know that I was not alone. That person, too, was a member of "the Club" and had been dealing with much more challenging issues than me during the same period. I had focused so inwardly on my own situation that I did not recognize this had been happening. Somewhere in the chemo fog, I recalled a conversation that I might have had about it. Those are, unfortunately, fleeting, sometimes fictitious, moments in my memory that haunt me from time to time. The incredibly moving conversation that day brought all kinds of emotions forward.

As I walked into the ward receiving room a week later, I was surprised to see my friend going in for treatment. It was the first time that our paths had crossed there, and I was glad that we had the opportunity to see each other. I entered the ward ten minutes later and chose to sit close to the restroom, which was always my preference. I did not make a big deal about my last treatment, but Denise's friend at the hospital acknowledged the fact right away.

I could tell that there was a different feeling among the staff, and for a moment, I thought that they just might be happy to see me go!

FEBRUARY 21, 2009

CHAPTER 58

PLANNING THE PIAZZA PLAQUE FOR ED FEIDNER

October 24, 2014

Thomas Sullivan
President
University of Vermont
85 South Prospect Street
Waterman Building
Burlington, VT 05405

Dear President Sullivan,

This letter is a little long; however, when I worked at Norwich University, I loved getting long letters from sixty-year-old alumni after homecoming, so I hope you will understand.

The 2014 UVM homecoming, specifically the Fortieth Reunion for the Royall Tyler Theatre, was memorable in many ways. I deeply appreciate the enthusiastic support that your office, the UVM Foundation, and the Alumni Office brought to the event to help the UVM Department of Theatre faculty and staff recognize this important anniversary. All of this could not have happened without your support. Thank you!

I wish that you and Leslie could have joined us for the Friday-night event at the magnificent home of Beth and Keith Gaylord '76. Even with months of advance planning and coordination, we could not have anticipated the genuine outpouring of affection and friendship that began to orbit early that evening and continued out of control throughout the weekend's events on campus. Our group members proved that they still have seasoned voices by singing dozens of songs from shows—with virtually no music or lyric sheets necessary.

Keith, Jonathan Bourne '76, and Kent Cassella '77 coordinated the event, and it included a superb gourmet-food truck that prepared cuisine to order, a clever option that worked beautifully for our guests. We enjoyed a retrospective slide show of productions from our era—a different selection from the luncheon video—and then shared in the excitement of the premiere of the video of *The Contrast*, which chose highlights from the remastered audio tape and long-forgotten photos—a truly significant addition to the university cultural archive that Gerry Hunt '74 sponsored and produced for this event. Topping the night was the presence of Mary Feidner, Betsy Schenk, and Gerry Moses, who are part of the fabric and history of the Royall Tyler Theatre. A great night! Or in the words of Ed Feidner, "Great! Just great!"

Over that past eighteen months, a group of 1970s theater alumni met monthly via teleconference to plan, fund, and coordinate aspects of our reunion. It was through this process that we discussed ideas and made suggestions to the department while relaying information via email, phone, letter, and social media to keep RTT alumni informed and up to date. We coordinated our efforts with the foundation and alumni offices and got tremendous support from Eileen Dudley and Sam Ankerson at every step along the way.

Alumni who attended—and some who did not—helped to fund the piazza plaque through sponsorship support and sale of the commemorative coins to other RTT alumni, theater faculty, and staff who wanted to participate. Our committee also oversaw the design, production, and delivery of the plaque, produced and distributed the commemorative challenge coin, promoted the event regularly with photos and other historical articles on Facebook, and produced two slide shows for the luncheon and RTT receptions, all at no additional expense to the department. The reunion inspired two photographers of our era—Charles Trottier and Heidi Racht—to donate their extensive show and candid photo archives to the university.

Keith made numerous trips to the theater and to special collections in search of files and records of our era. Most of these files remain elusive; however, we were able to bring together never-before-seen images of the time through personal collections. Keith's efforts also uncovered the historical archives of Dr. Bryan that represent significant work on the history of theater, not only at UVM but across America and Europe. Additional Bryan files were discovered at the theater in time to include in the department exhibit.

I simply cannot say enough about the events on campus Saturday—especially the luncheon that you and Leslie hosted for alumni and the Kushner interview. It is no surprise to us that the audience was predominantly from our era. Our classmates are always ready to come back to campus, enjoy each other's company, and share in the enthusiasm of the growth of the programs and the facility for a good cause. Everyone appreciated your comments and commitment to support renovations to the interior of the theater through a mini capital campaign this fall. I am sure that this will be accomplished and hope that the alumni contributions are matched in part by family contributions from the theater department faculty, staff, and parents— all essential elements in any capital campaign. The Kushner pledge of $1,000, as he held the silver challenge coin up high, inspired everyone and I hope will be used, as you suggested, to lead the way.

It overwhelmed me to see the changes on campus. For many of us, it was the first time we have walked around outside of the theater since our freshman year! It may sound strange, but that is how important that building and those productions were to us.

With all of the other extraordinary developments, I'd like to suggest that alumni buy a vowel and put STE(A)M in the future plans for UVM. I have spent the better part of the last three decades telling stories about combat engagements and the impact of war on our society and have spent most of the last decade building two military libraries. I turned recent attention to all manner of the arts and find that both are uniquely related. History and the preservation of rare documents, books, and artifacts are a major part of my DNA. This project highlighted for me that we are dangerously close to forgetting how the journey started and who took the first steps and neglecting to apply those ideals to the future. In the end, supporting the arts—all of the arts—is the highest priority.

The "Piazza Della Feidner" story is a simple one but highlights the love and respect that we had for the founders of the Royall Tyler Theatre and gave us all a chance to succeed or to fail. In 1974, Ed Feidner was forty-three years old—arguably the prime of his life. Despite consistent rumors of a medical condition, known or unknown, Ed would remain a champion of theater and the performing arts at UVM well into the new millennium. Bill Schenk and Dr. George Bryan brought balance and a range of experience to fulfill the mission—to make UVM theater and the Champlain Shakespeare Festival an integral part of the academic program at the university. It was all about engagement, participation, and professional stewardship that tapped into a large, willing group of students who were ready for any creative challenge.

If I had had more time at the luncheon, I would have told the story of the first rehearsal of *The Contrast* at the Royall Tyler Theatre during my sophomore year. Everything was new: the carpeting, the office furniture, the dressing rooms. The place was hot, dry, dusty, and loaded with static electricity.

I was cast in the chorus with a dozen other performers. There would be no permanent seats for several months, but no one seemed to care. We were curious and eager to please. Just being in this production was enough for every one of us. There was excitement everywhere. We were in awe!

Rehearsal started over winter break, so it was a big commitment to come back early and get started. But we could work all day—every day—on the production, which was a luxury for students with a heavy class load. After a short welcome by Ed Feidner, we gathered around our freshman musical director, Steve Freeman '77, and sang through the group numbers beginning to end. It was a little rough, but we had impressive sight readers, many of whom had been Vermont all-state and all–New England high school chorus participants. (Several in this talented group were also cast in *Covenant* a year earlier—the last show at the Arena Theater—and sight-read an impromptu a cappella performance of the "Hallelujah Chorus" during a break in rehearsal!) The theater was empty and hollow at first, still very much the gymnasium with a grid shadowed against the skylights, but the harmonies echoed throughout the building.

Midway through our first break, Ed Feidner pulled me out of the green room. Outside in the hallway, with Steve Freeman looking on, he told me that the actor cast as Van Rough had just quit the show. He thought that I could do the part and asked me if I would. As I said "Yes!" Ed turned back to the cast in the green room and immediately called everyone back in the theater, made the announcement of the change, and then asked me to step up and sing Van Rough's solo "Keep Your Little Eye Upon the Main Chance, Mary."

I had not even seen the song before. I was terrified. I walked up to the piano and realized that the skylights were now beaming down natural pools of light throughout the cavernous space. They would be covered in a few weeks, but at about eleven that morning, all of a sudden the light poured into the space. Thirty cast members watched with not a small amount of apprehension. Steve checked the key with me, and I began to sing the song full-out until all I could hear was my voice coming back from the back walls of the theater. It is the single most remarkable moment I ever had at the Royall Tyler Theatre, standing there in that awesome space, singing for the first time. In fact, I do not think I ever sang the song better than that first performance.

Theater training under Ed Feidner was a laboratory, and each of us was an experiment. We learned to react, adapt, and persevere while expanding our understanding of the world around us. We were compelled to work together as a team for a common goal that fostered confidence, pride, and a deep sense of belonging to a special, lasting, and, most importantly, unique outcome. The arts helped round us as individuals, providing purpose and a method to explore the creative voice we had inside. Drama, music, speech, and dance all thrive on the energy, enthusiasm, and passion of students at the precise time in their development that will influence the course of the rest of their lives. We were fortunate to have the freedom to explore and grow.

That is what happened to us forty years ago. That is why so many alumni were so eager to be back together and relive a little of that wonderfully creative experience we shared in the Royall Tyler Theatre. And that is why we are all still good friends today.

The group that helped support this effort includes more than forty alumni who gave what they could to be sure that the plaque recognition and other elements of the weekend were well represented. I will send a listing for Rich Bundy, Eileen Dudley, and Jeff Modereger, whose combined efforts in making this all possible are deeply appreciated by everyone who attended.

Thanks again to you and Leslie for making the weekend so enjoyable, and for dedicating valuable resources to support the social aspects of the reunion, the renovation, and the university theater staff in making this event a resounding success.

CHAPTER 59

PEOPLE I KNEW—
ROGER EBERT

Dear Roger:

Denise moved in a week ago Friday. Since then, we have shifted the accumulation of my life from closet and shelf to storage or Goodwill. In the middle of this process, I had to take a break from all of it due, in part, to your beautiful piece on Studs Terkel and my fascination with Buster Keaton.

Here is the brief but heartfelt story:

After the kitchen and clothes closets, my personal library, which seems to grow organically, presented my major challenge in combining lives at this time in life. During recuperation from the surgery, boxes of new books for our library programs were delivered and mixed with gifts from friends. Most of the more than 1,000 books in my collection have been moved to my office. The couple hundred that remain here have become almost unmanageable.

So, I had to make a decision and today was the day. I thought, as I started, "What would Roger do?" The answer was that you would put them in piles all around the house and enjoy them anytime you like. I tried that. Our condo is not big enough. Plan B: box, sort, store, and repurpose.

I first sorted books by topic and interest. I have an extensive collection of books about the New England–based photographer Wallace Nutting, whose hand-colored landscapes in the 1920s and 1930s are highly collectable. I have a few books on cast-iron cookware; many coffee-table books about Broadway, Hollywood, and Chicago; lots of sheet music; and even a growing and impressive collection of books by Roger Ebert.

By far, the collection of books about Buster Keaton takes up more shelf space than all the others and is the reason I am writing you today.

It is hard to sort through books without being compelled to open them and browse. Reconnecting with each one during the process is like visiting an old and dear friend. My worn and tattered paperback copy of Vonnegut's *Sirens of Titan*, which I always thought would be a great film, is literally falling apart—and still I cannot bear to part with it.

All this leads directly to you, Roger, and your wonderful remembrance of Studs Terkel, which I read several times throughout the day yesterday. While I have read his work and feel closer personally to him than I should, I've spent only about ten minutes with Studs Terkel in person. We discussed the subject of Buster Keaton in 2003, shortly after I moved to Chicago. I commended him on his two published interviews with Buster, and we shared a couple of moments talking about Buster and his wife, Eleanor, whom I worked with for several years on the musical project until her death in 1998.

To my ever-growing library on Buster, I've added signed copies of Studs' books that are in the work collection. But one recent gift from a good friend was *Buster Keaton Interviews* (2007 University Press of Mississippi//Jackson), edited by Kevin W. Sweeney. It came in the rush of post-operation sentiments and somehow missed my review pile. So, I was pleasantly surprised to open this book from the "Conversations with Filmmakers Series" and discover one of the interviews is Studs Terkel's 1960 interview.

In the introduction, Sweeney talks about the major interviews done with Keaton, and he cites the interview that I recall from Studs' book. Sweeney points out, however, that Studs published only a "condensed selection" from the entire interview at the time. So Sweeney went to the Chicago History Society (now "Museum") and transcribed the entire interview for publication in the book.

It is glorious. I stopped and spent some wonderfully enjoyable time sitting in the third chair as this nearly fifty-year-old conversation came to life in a whole new way for me. (Perhaps this is something that you have already read. If not, I'd be happy to send you a pdf, as I know one more book might tip the scales at home.)

Reading your piece in the *Sun Times* this weekend reminded me of all of this. I thought that it was curious that a book of interviews about filmmakers, with Studs' work beginning on page 108, would make this Sunday afternoon so satisfying and special.

I just thought you might like to know that what you do inspires people in many ways; some you might expect . . . and others that just happen with no explanation necessary.

SEPTEMBER 25, 2008

CHAPTER 60

DEAR JOHN—TREASURES

Dear John,

I have been thinking recently about all the different treasures in my life—things that enrich us in memory and experience the first time, and stimulate our understanding of the important things in life years later. We keep among the treasures gifts from special people, objects, sounds, and pictures that tell a story, and the experiences all summed lead us to a wonderful memory. The best treasure of all is the one that we imagine will come true.

Treasures from special people in our lives often find their next stop directly by intent—a mental note, or perhaps a written one, that guides a future decision. Many who admire art in a family home may find a note stuck on the back of that picture decades later from someone who thought that this would be just the right way to be remembered. Original art or rare books require mutual respect, admiration, and understanding of the artist or writer to become a treasure.

My mother was an artist, painter, poet, and musician. She must have had a beautiful singing voice at one time—I recall hearing it—but thyroid surgery dampened her abilities. So, she put her energy into playing songs from her youth on our old piano, short concerts that lasted twenty minutes or so, guided by sheet music from a seventy-year-old pile of frayed pages that had been played regularly during a time when that was the evening's entertainment.

She played Irving Berlin's 1925 classic "Always," which was played at her wedding, at each of her concerts. She would carefully position a delicate, frayed, and worn-on-all-edges early edition of the sheet music for playing and embellishment on our upright piano. Mom played a ballad with spirit, concentrating on all the notes, trying to make it look less mechanical. As she got older, and struggled to see and then play the notes in unison, her efforts were more for those around her than for herself.

I was mesmerized by piano music and my mother's performances and enjoyed applauding wildly. Most of all, I was taken with the genuine modesty she had for her wide-ranging talent.

On a visit years later at Christmas, I noticed the neglected pile of sheet music and started searching for any treasures I might recognize. Of course, the frayed copy of "Always" was there, crumbling in pieces as aged paper does. I found a file and stowed it carefully away, not thinking for a moment that it might be missed.

Back in New York, I contacted the Irving Berlin Music Company, who found and sent to me free of charge a newer copy of the sheet music, which I copied and had ready to deliver on my next trip home. What to do with the old, frayed version that had so many memories? How would that treasure be preserved? And almost no one was sure to play the new music—it was not the fashion anymore in our home.

And so, the framed "Always," with a miniature version of the new sheet music matted below, became my Mother's Day gift that May. My mom was elated. She admitted looking for the music one day recently and was saddened that she could not find it. She cheered when I played and sang it for her—the new music taking its new place in our home.

Years later, on May 11, 1988, at Carnegie Hall, I attended an event honoring Irving Berlin's 100th birthday with a star-studded roster of entertainers that included Shirley MacLaine, Frank Sinatra, Willie

Nelson, Bea Arthur, Michael Feinstein, Natalie Cole, Ray Charles, Marilyn Horne, and many others for the filming of a television special.

And everyone waited for Sinatra to sing "Always."

Taking his spot before the hushed crowd, Sinatra said he called Irving on his birthday every year, but on this special one, he wanted to sing the song that Berlin wrote for his wife of sixty-two years. What happened next is every performer's nightmare.

Sinatra proceeded to sing "Always" in a completely different key from the orchestra.

Despite attempts to mute instruments and adjust tempo, there was no turning back and no stopping this shockingly inharmonic performance. The audience was silent and numb throughout and applauded politely, with most thinking this might be the absolute end of Frank Sinatra's career at Carnegie Hall.

From stage right, the stage manager entered and whispered something in Frank's ear. He turned to the crowd and said, "They tell me there were technical difficulties with that last take. Would you folks mind if we try it again?" And with that, Frank Sinatra started all over again from the wings, except this time, of course, he nailed it.

I'm sure that my performance for my mother was better than Frank's first one by a long shot. I'd still take listening to one more rendition of my mom's. All these years later, the treasure that today rests on my wall, from time to time, recalls Irving Berlin, Frank Sinatra, and the story of my mother's wedding song.

Most object treasures become significant and cannot be made so. Christmas gifts can become immediate treasures for a lifetime. As children, we find it hard to separate the meaning of Christmas from the gift-giving. Parents play Santa to try to identify the one or two gifts that will simply bring joy.

On two occasions I received and lost object treasures—one within an hour; the other lost to time.

I was a Cub Scout and dedicated badge-earner in my troop. Our rural neighborhood promoted scouting, and our den mother was a good friend of my mom's. Her three boys were a pack unto themselves, but growing up, we all had a lot of fun together.

They had all the Cub Scout stuff as a rite of passage from one brother to the next. I had the basics, but always wanted one of those shiny Cub Scout pocketknives. So it was that one Christmas, under the tree, I found a brown-ribbed pocketknife with the official Cub Scout insignia on the side.

When you receive a treasure like this, two things come to mind: you want to use it immediately, and you do not want to lose it. I recall being protective of the knife, putting it in my front pocket and checking that it was there, taking it out and opening all of the four implements and showing everyone in the room how much it shined when opened in the sunlight.

I found a piece of leather lace and tied the knife to my belt loop. We were one.

I dressed in a hurry and headed for the barn, knowing that the next test would be to cut something.

"Don't cut off your finger" were the last words I heard from my dad as I raced out the door.

I did not, but I did manage to gash the middle finger of my left hand on the first piece of twine I grabbed to cut with the knife. Bloody, in tears, and racing back to the house, I would not need stitches, but I have a small scar to remind me of my first experience with that treasure. I never trusted myself with that particular knife, so I kept it in a very safe and secure place, the location of which I have long forgotten.

The scar, by the way, is on the same finger that was ripped open by a few remnants of gunpowder involved in a youthful experiment with the firing pin of a 12-gauge shotgun shell that is perhaps a story for another day.

Christmas 1965 brought one of the most cherished treasures ever—a Wham-O Super Ball. Every nine-year-old had a yo-yo and a Super Ball. It cost a little more than a dollar, but to me it was priceless.

I was so excited after opening the package that I grabbed my coat, put on my snow boots, and ran out to the shed, which iced over every year from the spring in our yard. I wanted to see the ball bounce off every wall, just like the commercial on television.

And did it ever. The first time I threw the ball, it banged off the walls, ceiling, old wooden boxes, rake handles, and hubcaps, and then miraculously rolled right back to my feet. The second time I threw it, I heard it hit a hubcap and a wall, and then it landed with a thud deep in the darkened cavern of the shed.

I spent the next hour frantically searching for my new treasure, but it was not to be found. My parents had little sympathy and decided that if I wanted another Wham-O Super Ball, I could save for it. I'm not sure why I decided it was not important, but that treasure was never replaced.

Decades later, and several months after my dad passed, the old shed was scheduled to be torn down. It had served only as a place to park the family car in recent years, with old tires, signs, wooden boxes, and hand tools accumulated on all sides. The spring had now created a muddy bog in one corner that consumed everything else around it.

In the process of cleaning up, I knew that a corner of the shed had a trove of old Coke and Fanta bottles from the 1950s and 1960s, and I salvaged several cases along with several other antique glass bottles. And there, among the clutter, was the brand-new, 1965 Wham-O Super Ball that sits on my desk today.

There are, of course, valuable, personal treasures that are handed down from generation to generation. My elation generated from the gift of my great aunt's wedding ring in no way offset the sadness in its accidental loss a few years later. It was, after all, a treasure that could not be replaced, a rare English-cut stone in a turn-of-the-century setting. I am reasonably sure that the actual engagement ring from my first marriage—a twisted piece of solder that was also lost for a while, but then found—still does exist somewhere in the possessions of my ex-wife. As I recall, the loss of that ring was offset by the joy in its finding.

Among the other treasures I savor: the sound of a train whistle that reminds me of the last day I saw my dad alive; the postcard bag from Paris that recalled a dream of a magical angling rod and a message to my granddaughter years before she was born; the cross-chain hook that was so worn from vibration on my dad's toolbox that the metal almost wore through; and the only piece of bronze casting that my mother ever completed: an elegant, curved ashtray.

I have been thinking recently about all the different treasures in my life—things that enrich us in memory and experience the first time, and stimulate our understanding of the important things in life years later. We keep among the treasures gifts from special people, objects, sounds, and pictures that tell a story, and the experiences all summed lead us to a wonderful memory. The best treasure of all is the one that we imagine will come true.

MARCH 2, 2012

Act II, Scene 6

Never falter
Never give up
Don't show your feelings
Just shoulder up

Nurse Nan
Act II, Scene 6

CHAPTER 61

ACT II, SCENE 6

SETTING: Waiting Room

SONGS: OUNCE OF PREVENTION
             LIVE YOUR LIFE

ON RISE: In one of two separate areas, SAM and
             KATHARINE are in mid-discussion.

KATHARINE is comforted by her father's courage but
concerned for the future.

Crossfade to NAN, TESS, and TOSS in a nearly
identical discussion about the outcome of recent
treatments. The news is encouraging.

NAN leads OUNCE OF PREVENTION.

MOTHER and JACK enter with KATHARINE and SAM; all
sing LIVE YOUR LIFE.

The COMPANY gathers and completes the musical number.

CHAPTER 62

THE MOST IMPORTANT RULE OF ALL

THE CHEMOTHERAPY TREATMENT ALWAYS starts with a blood test. I never thought much about those tests because all of mine had been good. On this particular day, when the tests came back good, I asked the nurses to explain to me what good was. They went into the technical description, and when that clinical haze came across my face, they simply assured me that my tests have always been within the parameters that they want to see.

As they prepared me for my final treatment, my friend—the one who had recently told me he had also been dealing, unknown to me, with cancer—walked by my chair. In all of my previous visits over six months, I had never known anyone personally in the ward. I looked up and asked if his treatment was complete. He replied that the blood test did not pass and he would have to come back next week.

Until that moment, I didn't know what the next step would be if the blood test failed. I did know that the expectation of each of these visits to the chemo ward requires a mental mindset that takes days to achieve. The disappointment of not taking one more step forward in battling this most challenging disease would be difficult to accept.

So, any jubilation that I might have felt from finally completing six months of chemotherapy and not having to return in two weeks for another session was tempered that day when I saw my friend leave unattended.

I have recently joined a special Club whose members continue to battle cancer. You play the cards you are dealt, remain positive, and make the most of every day you have. Each one of us in "the Club" knows that now, more than ever.

And, in our world, Rule No. 1 applies.

FEBRUARY 21, 2009

CHAPTER 63

PEOPLE I KNEW— WILLIAM E. COLBY

Editor's Note: In the last weeks of his life, former CIA director William E. Colby attended Norwich University's Military Writers' Symposium. Participants included W. E. B. Griffin, Philip Caputo, and others. It was perhaps Colby's last opportunity to reflect publicly on the role of the military.

WILLIAM COLBY LISTENED INTENTLY. He was eloquent and soft spoken, but he listened very well. It was one of his best qualities.

But the symposium was a chance for him to speak on a wealth of topics. For example, he discussed the unique challenges that future, localized military engagements will create.

"I think you'll have a problem of how to deal with very hostile populations in some areas. Terrorism. Riot. Fundamentalism. Hatred of different tribes, and we get in the middle of it because there is no one else there.

"And how do you work your way through that? How do you combine the forces of politics, of police, of information and of soldiers? Leave out the technology. How do you combine those forces to handle mobs? To handle crowds? How do you get your hostages out of situations they are in?"

Colby noted the growing threat of terrorist attacks and how the military would react. "We have some people working on that every day. It involves individual heroism. Going into hijacked planes from the rear with percussion bombs that go off. Stun the enemy and you go in and get the passengers out. All sorts of techniques along those lines."

Colby was critical of military spending, considering it too aggressive with no perceived threat, and suggested we seriously review or even realign our priorities.

Who's in Charge?

Colby is on a small stage in Northfield at Norwich University, the nation's oldest private military college, with major fiction writers and military historians.

Author W. E. B Griffin believes "the problem [of tomorrow's military] is going to be control of the actions of future forces. The State Department is getting involved, as is the CIA, in addition to the Army."

Colby agrees and gives an example on the development of policy in the White House. He credits President George Bush with piloting the process that "the president is supposed to say where he wants the war to take place and then let the soldiers take care of it." Decide, delegate, then disappear. Successful, but not particularly popular. Certainly politically terminal.

There is no doubt that this Bill Colby is the same one who parachuted behind enemy lines during World War II with the OSS; the same man who spent years in Vietnam; the same career operative who took to task the moral fiber of the CIA—and the nation's perceptions of covert operations.

Just two weeks before a tragic canoe accident would take his life, he is animated, jovial and at ease with any topic—from the "heroic myth" to four decades of political espionage.

The discussion turns to leadership for the troops in a technological age. He explains that the new era began in the Cuban Missile Crisis when the destroyer commander beside the Soviet ship carrying missiles was told by Bobby Kennedy and the White House to move 100 yards closer or 100 yards away.

"The Navy was horrified at that violation of the chain of command," Colby continues, "but in a sense, you have to say that destroyer commander should not be allowed to start World War III all by himself. So maybe there is some justification for tight control of a tough situation."

Hometown Boy

If you want to know who Bill Colby was, look at his upbringing and the influence of his father, a history professor at the University of Vermont. Consider Colby as a teenager, graduating from Burlington High School. If you asked him, he would say he was "just a hometown boy in these parts."

He lived by the motto that you had first to serve your country. Her interests. For her protection at all costs.

The necessity to operate secretly—something Colby admitted causes the American people to suspect that something is illegal—does not necessarily mean that you can or should randomly break the law. This particular value will be one of historical debate whenever Colby's name comes up.

Fact or Fiction

During the open forum, Joanne Holbrook Patton, the wife of General George Patton IV (also in attendance), asks what books military students should choose for the fact and fiction of leadership.

"Biographies are perhaps a good place to start," Colby answers. "Washington, Jefferson, Lincoln, Roosevelt. If you see what they have written and how they reacted to situations during their time, that is a lesson for the future."

Colby also mentioned *War and Peace* as a personal favorite, depicting the reality of conflict.

The Heroic Myth

As the discussion shifts ultimately to Vietnam, Colby listens as author Philip Caputo charges that our government suffered a lapse in mission in Southeast Asia. He questions whether, after Vietnam, there could ever again be "mythic heroes" about whom a future author could write. Colby counters that often throughout our history, our causes for war were flawed.

Colby cites our tactical strategy in World War II, in which Allied forces first chose manufacturing operations as bombing targets, gradually shifting to nonmilitary targets, then to the ultimate use of nuclear weapons. Countless lives were lost to "bring a swift and decisive end to the war."

Vietnam, however, is an era for which his generation has claimed ownership. "I have been critical of what we did there, but not why we were there," he says.

On the rules of engagement, Colby is clear: "You first must have a purpose. A hope of victory to justify the deaths that will inevitably occur. And you must have a strategy." He adds, "It was the failure of any true strategy until 1968 that perpetuated the war" that Caputo remembers.

History teaches us lessons, says Colby, and it was the lesson of Vietnam that provided success in Desert Storm. "The military were allowed to develop a sound strategy, and there was support from the president," he says.

The conference's final word on the "mythic hero" is also offered by Colby: "You need to have individual heroes—those who react to a terrible situation and respond at the risk of human life. You also have heroes at the general level, who have the ability to articulate the strategy for the best use of force involved. And also the political hero, who can articulate the purpose of the war to attract the support of the American people."

Colby was, unquestionably, all three.

MAY 20, 1996
BURLINGTON FREE PRESS

CHAPTER 64

NEMO STREET— AN EPISODE OF *THE TWILIGHT ZONE*

MAIN CHARACTERS:

Nick Slater—A forty-year-old man
Maddie Slater—Nick's fourteen-year-old daughter
Yetta Teerts—A spry, kind-looking, plainly-dressed
eighty-year-old woman

TIME: Twenty-four minutes

CUE: OPENING *THE TWILIGHT ZONE* THEME

Narrator:

"There is a fifth dimension beyond that which is known
to man. It is a dimension as vast as space and as
timeless as infinity. It is the middle ground between
light and shadow, between science and superstition,
and it lies between the pit of man's fears and the
summit of his knowledge. This is the dimension of

imagination. It is an area which we call the Twilight Zone." *(Actual show opening—Rod Serling)*

SCENE I: Spring on a crowded city street in an ethnic area of lower Manhattan, circa 2019. A man and his daughter walk down an urban street as the camera pans on them from left to right and above.

The two talk about the festival and the fun they will have, while the man, in a frenzy, looks at his cell phone for a specific building number. As he nears their destination, we see the sign over the door.

It reads "YETTA TEERTS EMPORIUM—*Palm Readings.*"

They enter.

PAN SHOT to NARRATOR on camera.

NARRATOR: "Nick Slater and his daughter, Maddie, have walked these Manhattan neighborhood streets for years. But on this bright, spring day, Nick searches for clues to their future. With little reason to hope that things will get better anytime soon, Nick decides to put his fate into someone else's hands.

"It's a decision that will lead him out of his own reality . . . and straight into the Twilight Zone."

CUE: THEME

SCENE II: The interior of Yetta's shop

Yetta's Emporium is a wonderous collection of curios designed to reflect peace and harmony. As Nick and

Maddie examine the artifacts in the room, Yetta emerges to greet them from one of several chairs in a grouping near the shop window and invites them to sit. Yetta tells them that they are on their way to the First World Festival, pointing to a decades-old carnival poster on the wall. Nick and Maddie are surprised that Yetta knows anything about it. Yetta tells them her story. She has been in the neighborhood, in the same location, for forty years, and she remembers seeing them walk by for the last ten years or so at this time of year and then returning home with festival gear later in the day, adding, "In my business, it pays to be observant."

There is something different this year, however. Yetta remembers a woman walked with them in the past. Nick explains that his wife, Ashley, Maddie's mother, died the summer before. Nick also discloses that he lost his marketing job two months prior, and that he has had a difficult time finding work of any kind. Maddie confesses that they may have to move out of their apartment. Nick admits that while they are making ends meet on unemployment, it will run out soon. They are stuck.

"Can't afford to stay," he says. "Can't afford to leave."

"So," Yetta says, "you have come here to Yetta Teerts Emporium, in search of a future?" Yetta motions for the two to lean in closer, takes one of each of their hands—one at a time—in hers, and studies it carefully. First Nick's. Then Maddie's. And then, back again to Nick.

Yetta says she feels the anxiety and pain that is present in both of them. It clouds their own ability to look forward positively. She sees so much grief present in their relationship that it is difficult to determine what the immediate course will be.

With hopefulness, Yetta tells them that soon, however, an opportunity will present itself. It will be a momentary decision and one that they must immediately commit to for their situation to improve.

Despite questions by Nick for specifics, Yetta is unable to provide any more information. Maddie is skeptical. Nick rises to leave and offers to pay. Yetta refuses the money, and then gives Maddie a gift—a tiny compact mirror—that is on display. Maddie is thrilled, and thanks Yetta, and they leave the shop.

SCENE III: Back on the street

Nick and Maddie leave the shop and walk down the street to the subway stair entrance. Nick is confused and despondent. Maddie tries to cheer him up as they take the escalator into the subway.

SCENE IV: A modern subway station

Nick and Maddie emerge from the escalator as the subway car loads up. The station name, "BARKLEY AVENUE," is embedded in large, bold letters into the tiles on the station wall.

SCENE V: On a subway train

Nick and Maddie take a seat in a car that is half
full of riders. As the train pulls out of the
station, Maddie tells Nick that the stop for the
festival is "LONGE AVENUE," and that it is either
the second or third stop on the train.

The train pulls up to the next station. They hear
an announcement: "This is BAYVIEW. Next stop: LONGE
AVENUE." Nick and Maddie rise and stand at the door
of the train, talking about what they will do first
at the festival. Nick leaves his cell phone, which
has fallen out of his pocket, behind on the seat.

SCENE VI: A subway platform

As they continue their conversation, the train pulls
up to the station, the doors open, and Nick and
Maggie are the only passengers to depart.

Laughing and still consumed with their conversation,
Nick and Maddie watch the train pull away and
turn to see that the subway platform is deserted.
Looking up together, they see the name "NEMO STREET"
embedded in large, bold letters into the tiles
on the station wall. Nothing looks familiar, and
confusion and fear wash over both Nick and Maddie
as they realize they have made a mistake. Nick
reaches for his cell phone, and it is not there.
Realizing that they got off at the wrong stop, and
now distraught about losing his phone, Nick panics.
Maddie lightens the moment by telling her father
that Ashley had always been the family navigator.
Nick agrees and then says the phone was an old model
anyway, so they relax and decide to sit on the bench
to wait for the next train to come.

PASSAGE OF TIME: A pan up to the digital clock adjacent to the sign shows the passage of time from 11:15 a.m. to 11:30 a.m. Then 11:45 a.m.

Seated on the bench as before, Nick decides that the train will not be coming and surmises that they must be close to the festival anyway. So, both decide to walk the rest of the way.

Looking around, there appears to be only one exit: a long, concrete corridor, with no escalator, leading to a stairway to the street at the far end. They approach the stairs and start to walk out of the station.

SCENE VI: Street level exit—rural setting

Nick and Maddie appear from the darkened exit doorway into bright, blinding sunlight. They are in the middle of a rural neighborhood square, unlike anything in their current time and place. The tree-lined street around the square is freshly paved. There are vintage cars everywhere, flowers grow in planters, and children run in a park nearby. There is nothing to suggest a specific decade or time, except that one might envision it to be the mid-1950s.

Along Nemo Street, where the shops line the square, there are traditional, well-kept businesses—Mack's Deli and Ice Cream Parlor; Locks Barbershop/Salon; Zell's Hardware—and a flurry of people moving about. To Nick and Maddie, the scene along Nemo Street is unrecognizable.

Down the sidewalk, people greet Nick and Maddie, smiling and saying a familiar "Hello," until the

pair arrives at Nora's Dress Shop, which has a
girl's dress in the window on sale for $14.95.

The beautiful dress catches Maddie's eye. As she
examines the merchandise, Nora, the store proprietor,
appears at the doorway and addresses both by name.
Nick is quizzical and asks her how she knows them.
Nora laughs it off and tells him to stop kidding
her. "Everyone knows you on Nemo Street," she says.
"The Slater Family General Store is an institution.
Are you feeling well, Nicholas Slater?" Nora then
looks to Maddie and tells her the blue dress would
look great on her, and she'll knock off $2, if she
wants it.

Nick, getting nervous, thanks Nora and motions to
Maddie that they need to keep walking. But a group
of people forms around them at the store window. A
finely dressed woman gives Nick a big hug and a kiss
on the cheek that leaves a pronounced lipstick mark.

Maddie starts to engage with the woman about the
dress as a man joins them and talks to Nick about
an order that will come into the store in a week
or so. He has been extended credit at Slater's and
wants Nick to know how much he appreciates Nick
giving him a break.

Two boys Maddie's age come out of the ice cream
shop, wave, and say, "Hi!" to Maggie.

Bewildered by all the attention, Maddie begins to
get nervous and moves closer to Nick. When Nick asks
one of the people where the store is, they tell him
half-jokingly, "Right around the corner on the left,

where it's always been." With that, Nick brushes off everyone around him, grabs Maddie's hand, and starts to walk in the other direction, back to the subway station.

SCENE VII: Subway station

Nick and Maddie head down the stairs and start to run through the corridor as they hear the train pulling into the station in the distance. Nick and Maddie reach the station platform just as the train pulls to a stop. Maddie points out that Nick has lipstick on his cheek from the kiss and gives him her compact mirror to see for himself. As Nick rubs the lipstick off his cheek, he sees something startling in the mirror as the train doors begin to open.

Maddie begins to enter the train car, but Nick pulls her back. Confused, Maddie asks what he is doing. Nick points at the reflection in the mirror of the station sign, "NEMO STREET." In reverse, it reads, "TEERTS OMEN." We then see the same reflection of the sign in the massive stainless-steel hood of the train as it pulls out of the station.

Nick and Maddie hug each other and then walk down the corridor toward the stairway as the NARRATOR is heard:

"If you haven't been to Slater's General Store recently, there's a new look to the business.

Welcoming spring in the neighborhood, Nick and Maddie Slater have turned their popular general store on Nemo Street into a cozy retreat that

welcomes everyone looking for a second chance in
life. It's right around the corner on the left, just
a short stop away from the Twilight Zone."

CUE: THEME

Act II, Scene 7

The cards you're playing
are a bad hand of canasta.
It's the Gorilla . . .
It's the Gorilla in the Room

Joe Gorilla & Company
Act II, Scene 7

CHAPTER 65

ACT II, SCENE 7

SETTING: Boardroom

SONGS: HOPE
             GORILLA IN THE ROOM
             THE CLUB (WE'RE IN)

Lights up on a loud and raucous boardroom. In
addition to the members, there are guests, staff, and
patients present, including the IMPATIENT PATIENT.
There are charts, graphs, and piles of reports.
Everyone has an opinion and appears animated. CHUCK
and JOE are prominent among the group.

With their bodies hidden from view, the CHAOSALS'
heads are displayed among the books on the
bookshelves.

The CHIEF has a new green chart with income trends
up and a solution icon to the long-term dilemma.
CHUCK endorses the CHIEF. In the course of the
presentation, the CHIEF and CHUCK present a plan to
save the center, reprising HOPE with the ENSEMBLE.

The CHIEF, who now sees JOE for the first time, asks, "When did you get here?"

"I have never left," JOE replies.

CHUCK and the CHIEF announce that the center has received two commitments for the future. The first is a $500M pledge that will be paid over five years; the second is a bequest that could amount to five times that amount upon the passing of the center's benefactor, the IMPATIENT PATIENT, introduced as Mr. Thadeous Metterant. The CHIEF attempts to hug Metterant and is promptly whacked by the cane.

An ORDERLY wheels out the IMPATIENT PATIENT as JOE hands the letter and check to CHUCK.

The CHAOSALS struggle to get free from the bookcase, but JOE waves them off and they disappear, replaced by potted plants.

JOE leads the COMPANY in GORILLA IN THE ROOM as principals gather their belongings to ride the elevator to the lobby and leave the center. One by one, the cast members pass on the street as in the beginning—an anxious couple hailing a cab, a woman with a stroller, business executives and service employees.

The CHIEF and THOMPSON leave last with the ORDERLY and the IMPATIENT PATIENT, who, together, rearrange the letters of the "TREATMENT CENTER" sign to spell "METTERANT CENTER."

BLACKOUT

During curtain call, the cast reprises THE CLUB (WE'RE IN). The actors playing JOE and THOMPSON address the audience. The actors provide current percentages of families impacted by a cancer diagnosis, treatment, and aftercare. It is announced that a portion of all the proceeds of every production of GORILLA IN THE ROOM provides funding for cancer research, treatment and family support services. "The running total, since opening night, is estimated at more than $XXXXXX."

At curtain, THOMPSON announces, "If you would like more information or to make a contribution to support this effort, please visit the website or see a member of the cast in the lobby following the performance. Thank you!"

CHAPTER 66

OF COURSE YOU DID

'Tis better to have loved and lost
than never to have loved at all.

Alfred Lord Tennyson

I MOST CERTAINLY HAD early-stage colon cancer when I moved to Chicago in 2002. The kind of cancer I was dealing with grows slowly and can go undetected if you are unsure of family history or do not recognize the warning signs.

Looking back, cancer was in many ways inevitable for me. I smoked two packs of cigarettes a day for twenty years, drank alcohol to excess, exercised infrequently, walked nowhere, skipped meals, worked constantly, postponed vacations, slept erratically, lost my sense of humor and with it my ability to enjoy life, and very nearly lost everything else important to me.

As a young man, I fell in love often and hard. If you knew me then, I was always concerned about the end game of a relationship, worried that I would hurt someone, be hurt myself, or end up smothered and unable to do the things I wanted to do. All that thinking got in the way of realizing that I was happier living in the moment than worrying about tomorrow.

I was equal parts charming, selfish, delightful, self-centered, talented, and arrogant. You realize, of course, that all of those qualities mean nothing when someone does break your heart—to the point that you think you can't ever repair it again.

But, of course, you do.

It happens to everyone. Your heart still functions. You do love again. You think you might never reach the same sustained, innocent, extraordinary level of passion you recall, when your toes curled and your body ached for more.

But, of course, you do.

And then there was the relationship that, every time she was in the room, my heart beat out of my chest with excitement. Little did I know then that I was on the verge of a massive coronary at the time that drugs have helped counterbalance since 2001.

In the end, Tennyson was right. I have no regrets about the life choices I have made because we become better people only if we allow others to see who we really are. I cannot change all the mistakes I made. I can only try to make myself a better human being today and tomorrow. That is a relatively new philosophy—a promise I made to myself at various times during my recovery period and the twelve years that have passed.

And while I would like to take credit for this as some sort of epiphany or self-realization, I had a bit of help. Spoiler alert: A cancer diagnosis is a game-changer.

One doctor actually told me at the time that I was fortunate.

"It will be easier to deal with colon cancer as a significantly obese white male," he said. "You'll lose all this weight and everyone will say you look great!"

There was a lot of truth in what he said. For a time, I joked about it, too. But it brought little comfort. I did lose the weight, and thanks for trying to cheer me up, Doc.

What I didn't count on is the effect that a colon cancer diagnosis and years of treatment would have on the sunset of my professional career, my relationships with everyone in my life, and, most curiously, my memory. Everything changed permanently. Less charming. More selfish. Never delightful at all. I became single-mindedly self-centered with diminishing patience, waning talent, and a level of arrogance that bordered on just plain mean. No matter how I tried to hide these feelings, those around me saw the change as well.

If you throw in the days I wasted feeling sorry for myself or not being able to stand the mix of body odor, sweat, and chemicals coming out everywhere, it's hard to imagine that anyone would ever again find me the least bit attractive or want to stay by my side.

I was, at that moment in my life, blessed. There was someone who was very, very good for me. She accepted my failures as a person. My changes in attitude. She gave me the benefit of the doubt, ignored my shortcomings and hostilities. All of them. Most of all, she forgave me for letting her down. She restored my soul and gave me confidence and hope.

I learned that if your heart is already on the mend, you can fill the rest with someone else's love for the person you will become. That person may be more cautious, caring and understanding, although none of these particular traits can be used when describing a chemotherapy patient. Whatever happens, as the *Wicked* lyric says, you "have been changed for good."

Every cancer patient I have known has the same inner feelings to one degree or another: a little bitter about the hand they were dealt; tired of feeling tired; and not always ready to accept the outpouring of concern that healthy people want to send their way. When cancer patients feel good, it's okay; when we don't, nothing really helps.

Above all, I made a decision early on that I did not want my cancer to define me, so I became a cancer fighter.

So, for no particular reason or with any goal in mind, I decided to write when I felt up to it to try to explain what was happening along the way. To my surprise, the introduction of cancer-fighting drugs in my system allowed me to recall very specific and lasting impressions of experiences throughout my life, and the lessons learned all flooded back at the same time. It became a little game I played every so often. It was fun. I looked forward to it and I was good at it.

So, this collection of essays, letters and other writings is the result of looking back, looking forward, and, from time to time, living precisely in the moment, which is, in the end, the best place to be. It is meant to inspire others to face the challenges in their own lives, live with and learn from their mistakes, practice forgiveness, cherish accomplishments no matter how small, and remember to respect and honor the people who had faith in them along the way.

There are in these pages personal reflections about people I knew, either from my own observations or, in some cases, in their own words. I taped and transcribed interviews with only minor editing for clarity. If comments are in quotes, they are word-for-word as best as I can recall. Often, I wrote memorandums following a visit or phone call so that I would remember details. Letters included here are only lightly dusted.

These are stories of my own, a reflection of life as I saw it, and of the people who helped through the journey.

JUNE 30, 2020

CHAPTER 67

LETTER FROM HELEN E. TRACY TO PAUL E. TRACY

Dear Paul:

Just some thoughts I wanted to share with you . . .

A Sunday ago, a bright and beautiful day, I was outside cleaning and picking up, when, with the bright sun reflecting, I saw a bottle shining on the bank by the house. In picking it up, I noticed it was an aged old vodka bottle. Immediately, memories came with a rush—pictures in my mind of that day as they always will be.

The picture, most vivid, of you—angry, frustrated, emptying the bottle and furiously heaving it up the bank; remembering the torment in my body and mind, suffering and begging you for just a little—to stop the shaking and pain. You then sitting quietly beside me, beginning to understand, your love, rising above the anger, frustration, and helplessness. Because of the love showing through that day, you used your strength and courage to seek help for me . . . for a problem that might have left the family shattered and me lost forever. The caring started that day touched many people within the family, uniting them together in the rocky, hard path back. I would never have made it without the support and strength I received. It can all be traced to a beginning, and that day was the beginning through love.

I have many pictures in my mind and heart, some so happy and beautiful. Some sad and lonely, and others black and ugly. But of all pictures, I will keep special that day and just pause and think— keeping it evergreen, for you see I must remember how it was, to appreciate and give thanks for how it is.

Each day becomes more important than the last, and places in my heart are thawing from the blackness, and I feel growth.

We have always been so very close, my son, and at this moment, reliving that day, I feel as if I never had been closer.

Had to share this with you,

Love Always,
Mom
Date Unknown

REFLECTIONS—FRIED OYSTERS ON A RAINY DAY

THERE ARE A FEW things you remember about a rainy day . . . the sudden change in cloud formation as the storm rolls forward . . . the ominous darkness that descends upon you . . . the urgency to find cover . . . or the need to brave the driving rain by escaping from one destination to another. Each of us has a mission when it rains. We must soldier on in spite of what is put before us, stay put until it passes, or, simply pay attention so that it doesn't pass us by without us noticing.

Something happened to me a year ago today that made me stop and appreciate the important things in life, as well as in the lives of those around me. On this day in 2008, following a routine colonoscopy, I learned that I had stage 3C colon cancer. That story, and the process over the past year to get back in the game of life, has been the subject of many essays. I was reminded of the date today, and the memories all came flooding back—over fried oysters on a rainy day.

You see, today is also the six-month anniversary of my wedding to Denise, and we have spent the last several days with my family. Much was made about everyone's news, and I was particularly opinionated about global affairs, politics, and various other issues. Maybe it was because my family was so interested in our work in Chicago and the attention to history and respect for the citizen soldier we carry in our daily lives in that venture.

Or perhaps it is because my friend John Callaway passed suddenly last week, and I will not have the pleasure of hearing his voice and views on this issue or that one ever again.

My family loved being together—they were proud of each other, their families, and their careers—and we genuinely had fun. It was a special day to see the cousins all grown up and making babies of their own. All of a sudden, my generation was not moving the chairs and making the decisions anymore. We could sit back and enjoy each other's company.

I sneaked away, for a time, to cast a fly on Lake Champlain. Anyone who fished at this resort would have told me it was a waste of time and that there was no way I was going to catch anything in the water that day. But no one around me said a word. Only I knew it was more about casting a fly than catching anything.

Considering the lingering effects of chemotherapy, I didn't know if I'd be able to tie a fly. I also did not know where to go. So imagine a floundering angler, carrying his gear bag and rod case up and down a fenced-in shore looking for an entry point along a steep cliff.

Eventually, I came upon a natural rock stair to the shoreline where a woman and two children—a girl and a boy—explored the rocks and landscape of the shore.

I was an enormous mystery to the children, who hovered over me as I carefully assembled the rod, attached the reel, and then went about selecting the proper fly to tie. The young boy, in particular, was curious about the flies, and he asked if they were "real" and did I think I'd really catch a fish. I belied my insecurity, but it took me a long time to tie the fly on the line as I tried to manage my composure with all the questions. Once that was done, I stood tall on a jutting rock, double-hauling with all my strength in a remarkably vain attempt to cast into a steady breeze.

I realized quickly that I would have had better luck with a club than a fly rod. With the wind picking up and a combination of rolling surf and low water level, it was turning into a futile exercise.

The children, however, were enthralled. They watched the steady improvement of my casts. And as the tempo surged back and forth, I noticed an eagerness as they waited for a fish to rise to my fly in the choppy waters. It felt like I had a captive audience, so I tried harder to make every cast perfect.

At some point, every angler knows that fly fishing becomes more about being there than catching anything. I think that is the essence of fishing in general. On this day, I achieved the ultimate goal—to prove, in some small way, that I had the physical dexterity to tie a fly to a line and cast in the open air.

After a while, one odd thought crossed my mind: the realization that, for that moment, I was not part of the family gathering. I was isolated and apart. I then wondered if anyone had noticed that I was not there. Or that I had left at all.

"Are they missing me?" I thought.

Once I realized that I was gone, I felt great urgency to return. Having proved that I could fish, I convinced myself that it seemed pointless to continue.

I turned and discovered that I was completely alone. Even my child audience had departed.

So, I abruptly packed my gear away and walked back up the rocky stairs to the lodge. When I returned to the party, there was so much chaos with kids running around that no one noticed. So, I settled down in a shady chair and immediately drifted off into a peaceful nap. When it came time to eat, I was roused awake and gave everyone the rundown on the fishing excursion.

And I told my family how much it meant to me that we had all been together on such a glorious day.

Today—a year after this all started—I realize that I have spent an enormous amount of my life planning and executing all sorts of programs that may or may not make the world a better place to live. Along the way, there have been extraordinary highs and devastating lows, each one challenging and invigorating. The personal rhythm of the last week, however—from Father's Day to today—has been particularly turbulent and unlike any week in a long time.

At the end of this week—on this special day—it rained like the sky was crying. It stopped, and then came back with similar fury: cascades of water churning forward, people running for cover and darting in and out, trying to avoid a single drop.

This is all logical to me: the rain always gave way to a calm in the center of the storm and the promise of another deluge to follow. All predictable. If you are patient, the rain will pass and you will be spared any inconvenience.

That was not my choice, and never has been, so out in the storm's fury I went, not waiting for another moment to pass by unconsumed.

There are a few things you remember about a rainy day . . . the sudden change in cloud formation as the storm rolls forward . . . the ominous darkness that descends upon you . . . the urgency to find cover . . . or the need to brave the driving rain by escaping from one destination to another. Each of us has a mission when it rains. We must soldier on in spite of what is put before us, stay put until it passes, or, simply pay attention so that it doesn't pass us by without us noticing.

Something happened to me a year ago today that made me stop and appreciate the important things in life, as well as in the lives of those around me . . . like running headlong into the rain . . . sending a few satisfying casts into the wind . . . or sharing fried oysters on a rainy day.

JUNE 30, 2009

GORILLA IN THE ROOM

LOGLINE

Members of a special club join together to
overcome a formidable foe.

GORILLA IN THE ROOM is a book musical about four families
dealing with cancer. The story takes place in and around a twenty-
first-century urban treatment center, the admissions and office areas,
and the hospital chemotherapy ward.

Casting | Character Notes: The title character, Joe Gorilla, may
be cast as Jane Gorilla or J. Gorilla. Diversity is encouraged and
standards of the *Bechdel Test* apply. The Chaosals (pronounced *KAY-
AH-SOLS*, as in those who raise chaos and havoc) are playful, unseen
disrupters at the treatment center. It is vital to the development of
the story that Joe and his Chaosals appear to be off-center, confusing
and diabolical in their opening scenes, but are never mean to anyone,
especially patients and caregivers. Over the course of the play, the
Chaosals appear and disappear as if by magic until we realize that
they are gone for good. It is then that Joe's actions emerge as spirited
challenges all along to continue a fight for survival and hope. *et*

CHARACTERS
(In Order of Appearance)

Patients and Family

Katharine Hines . . . . Daughter of Cancer Patient Sam—
Mid-thirties

Jack . . . . Katharine's Fiancé—Mid-thirties

Sam Hines . . . . Cancer Patient/Marine Veteran—
Mid-seventies

Tess Terone . . . . Cancer Patient (Non-Spiritualist)—
Mid-twenties

Toss Terone . . . . Twin Sister of Tess (paternal or
identical)—Mid-twenties

Mother Terone . . . . Mother of Terone Twins

Colin Mason . . . . Cancer Patient—Mid-forties

Jill Mason . . . . Colin's Spouse—Mid-thirties

Megan . . . . Daughter—Teenager*

Major Clint Baker, USA . . . . . . Army Medical Corps—Mid-
thirties*

Edison Brown . . . . Clint's Partner/Cancer Patient—
Mid-thirties

Hospital Staff

Dr. Roy Thompson . . . . Oncologist

Chief . . . . Chief Administrator

Nurse Nan/Shepard . . . . Head Nurse/Oncologist Assistant*

Wilson . . . . Orderly/Attendant*

Chuck . . . . Board Chair

*Ensemble**

The ensemble is comprised of eight actors who double and understudy roles of social workers, therapists, clinicians, window washers and board members.

Featured

Thadeous Metterant . . . . The Impatient Patient
The Chaosals (*KAY-AH-SOLS*) . . . . Joe's impish sidekicks
Joe Gorilla . . . . The Gorilla in the Room

GORILLA IN THE ROOM

S O N G   S U I T E

ACT I
A Late-Fall Day—Present

The Club (We're In)	Katharine, Tess, Toss, Colin, Edison
Gorilla in the Room	Joe, Chaosals
Chemotherapy Sucks	Sam, Edison, Jill & Chorus
Hope	Katharine, Jack, Clint, Jill
I Wish There Was A Way (To Say This Differently)	Thompson, Tess, Toss, Nurse Nan
What's a Mother to Do/ What My Mother Said	Mother Terone & Katharine
Just a Day in the Blue Room	Joe, Chaosals, Nurse Nan, Chorus
Chemo Brain	Impatient Patient
Too Much Information	Chief Administrator
Big Business	Chief, Board Members
This Is What I'd Do with a Tomorrow	Edison, Clint, Colin, Jill, Sam & Company

ACT II
Early Spring—Six Months Later

She's A Fine Old Girl (She Is)	The Window Washers
All Those Good Things (That We Had)	Tess, Toss, Mother
All Those Good Things (Goin' Bad)	Joe, Chaosals, Chorus
How Is He (What About Me)	Clint, Katharine, Jill, Megan
Home/ Holidays	Sam, Thompson
The Examination	Nan, Joe, Thompson
Busy Busy, Very Busy	Chief, Joe, Chorus
What My Mother Said (Reprise)	Katharine
Ounce of Prevention/ Live Your Life	Nurse Nan, Tess, Toss, Katharine, Sam
Hope (Reprise)	Chief, Thompson & Company
Gorilla in the Room (Reprise)	Joe & Company
The Club (We're In) (Reprise)	Company

ACKNOWLEDGMENTS

THE CONTRIBUTIONS AND INSPIRATION of so many friends and colleagues to this project—many members of "the Club" themselves—is only fractionally surpassed by the expert care and treatment of the medical professionals I observed over the past twelve years. Choosing to remain positive and curious about the stories of others—some told here within and some not—has expanded my ability to accept our differences as human beings and understand that in order to exist, we all are required to both listen and to be heard. It is a delicate balance to be sure.

Although the names of those medical professionals directly involved in my care have been changed in the body of this work, their initials follow to recognize them for their expertise, then and now, and as a tribute to all health workers who have been on the front lines during the COVID-19 pandemic. Thank you: AMB, ALK, JBM, SNN and SJS. The depth of my gratitude to the late Dr. Patti Tighe cannot be measured.

Special thanks to two old friends: my heartfelt appreciation to Frank Sesno for his exceedingly kind and thoughtful foreword; and to artist and illustrator James Dietz, who created the whimsical cover illustrations of Times Square from the germ of the idea that inspired the musical within the book.

Over the years I have had the honor to explore thousands of individual stories within the life experiences and writings of historians, combat veterans and Medal of Honor recipients. Many of the stories within this volume would not have been possible if not for the friendship and encouragement of: Jeff Shaara, William E. Butterworth IV, Jack Jacobs, Nick Kehoe, H. R. McMaster, Shirley and Carlo D'Este, David Bellavia, Joe Galloway, Phil Caputo, Elizabeth N. Norman, Neil Hanson, Paul Stillwell, Hershel W. Williams, Gary Johnson, Dave Moody, Dixie and Sammy Davis, Charles W. Newhall III, Sally Shelton Colby, Paul Colby, the late W. E. B. Griffin, and Winston Groom, who passed as we were preparing for publication.

Thanks as well to many others who heard, and in some cases read, versions of these stories along the way: John Zukowsky, Mark Roderer, Mary Feidner and her daughters, Julie and Beth, Liz Ingoldsby, André De Shields, Michael Popowski, Diana Weggler, Gary Johnson, Jaime and Rich Schneider, Chaz Ebert, Chris DeSantis, Barbara LaSpesa and Seymour Zitomersky, Henry Godinez, Monique Sattler, Peder Dahlberg and Gloria Balague, Cathy Metcalf, Robin and Ken Gilman, Heidi Kettenring and David Girolmo, Kayla Boye, Lauren and Thom Cooper, Kenny Raskin, Lauren Wobby, Margaret Hedberg, John Riggi and David Wendelman, Ross Howarth, Edward Gero, Melissa Jestes, Colleen Loughlin and John Sirek, Robert Mack, Kimberly Miller, Howard Reich, Rhona and Julian Frazen, Bill Larkin, John Michael Downs, Joyce Owens and Monroe Anderson, Paul Marinaro, Megan Bueschel, Brenda Didier, Michelle Durpetti, Dave Linden, Gene Garcia, Harvey Calden, Dan Thompson, Patti Larsen, Elaine Dame, Robin and Dan Moulton, Karl Grupe, Trey Spencer, Ellen Hart, Wendy Finch, Betsy Jackson Marshall, Greg Sanders, Mary Swann, Barbara Dallas, Howard Lincoln, Betsy Schenk, Jerry Freund, Peter Cooley, Jan Nickel, Robert Hodierne, Stephanie Juckem, Kate Linsner, Robert Sims, Tamara and Jay Sims, Joe Schofield, Steve Wright, Allen Shechtman, Ken Baker, Christine Vande Voort, Donica Lynn, David Rosenberg, Jim Frazier, and all of the Petterino's Monday Night Live family, a vast list that includes: Beckie, Irwin, Tom, Jay, Joan, Bob, Cynthia, Cheryl, Carla, Larry, Judy, Bernie, Nick, Scott, Marty, Carl, Jeannie, Abigail, Marianne, Laura, Carmen, Tammy, Lou, Russ, Denise, Sophie, Vasily, Michael, Sandee, Polly, Peg, Kurt, Paw Paw, the good folks at Tables 1 and 2, and cast members from more than a hundred shows who stopped by Booth 23 to say hello over the years. The contributions of Dr. J. Kim Worden, a consummate storyteller and former University of Vermont professor, are immeasurable.

I am blessed with deep personal ties to UVM theater classmates all these years later, a network that includes: James Kowal, Steve Freeman, Peter Delorenzo, Brooke, Stacey and Lisa Gladstone, Jonathan Bourne, Hamilton Gillett, Sarah Brooke, Josh Conescu, Kent Cassella, Peter Kurth, Melonie Donovan, Keith Gaylord, Laurel Casey, Craig Toth, Adam Zahler, and F. Patrick Orr. There are many more of the mid-'70s era, and the decades that followed, who have stayed in touch and burned away hours during the pandemic reading Shakespeare and rekindling memories of days gone by. I hope they find these stories familiar and satisfying.

Gorilla in the Room and Other Stories would not have been possible without the expert guiding hand of Kelly Kennedy, whose organizational and editorial skills are all over this book. Although publication was delayed several months due to the pandemic, we were able to keep the project on schedule thanks to Kelly's expertise and enthusiasm.

I am very grateful for my longstanding association with John Koehler and Koehler Books who, with Joe Coccaro and Kellie Emery, have enthusiastically guided this project with care and consideration at every step along the way. It has been my pleasure and privilege to work with Koehler's senior editor, Hannah Woodlan, in preparing the book for publication. Thank you!

After collaborating for almost twenty-five years with Lori Ames on other projects, I am grateful and excited to have her leading the team at ThePRFreelancer, Inc. in the promotion of this one.

I would not be an angler today without the OAFS—Barry Meinerth, Yank Shugg and Robert Plumb. We have had countless adventures together. This small brotherhood carried my bags at a time when my head was yearning for an escape, but my body was struggling to keep up. They taught me that when you have friends like this on the hook, reel them in and keep them close. *Tight Lines!*

Understanding that it is as fulfilling to love as it is to be loved may be the most important lesson of all. And in these isolating times, the thoughts, images and conversations with my daughter, Amanda, and my granddaughter, Allie Kate, bring me great joy. I dream endlessly about the moment we can hold each other again.

I am so thankful for the patience, humor, and love of my wife, Denise. She is my world, and at this most critical time, we depend on each other more than ever before.

Despite the devastating impact of the pandemic to the performing arts, the restaurant and event-planning industry, the artistic community of producers, directors, designers, actors, musicians, stage managers, costumers, technicians, makeup artists, front-of-house staff, publicists and, yes, theater critics, I remain hopeful and optimistic for the swift return of the exhilaration and electricity of an opening night audience and the deafening sound of a resounding curtain call.

See you on the other side of the aisle.

Ed Tracy
October 20, 2020

ABOUT THE AUTHOR

ED TRACY IS AN award-winning broadcast veteran, writer, editor, and host of *Conversations with Ed Tracy*, a Chicago-based cultural series of thoughtful and engaging discussions with authors, performing artists and other arts-based leaders. Tracy was the founding executive director, and later president and CEO, of the Pritzker Military Library in Chicago that received the 2009 National Medal for Museum and Library Services and was recognized five times by the Webby Awards for outstanding programming, including *Pritzker Military Presents* and *Medal of Honor with Ed Tracy*. A recipient of a Chicago Midwest Regional Emmy Award and the Norwich University Board of Fellows Service Medallion, Tracy is a graduate of the University of Vermont with a bachelor of arts degree in theater and communications, and a member of the American Theatre Critics Association, the National Press Club, and the American Society of Composers, Authors and Publishers (ASCAP). *Gorilla in the Room and Other Stories* is his first book.

Review platform
PicksInSix®
Website
conversationswithedtracy.com
gorillaintheroom.com

ABOUT THE CONTRIBUTORS

James Dietz/Cover Art

THE ACCLAIMED ARTIST/ILLUSTRATOR James Dietz was born in San Francisco and attended Art Center College of Design in Los Angeles. He now lives & works in Seattle, Washington with his wife Patti and his wonder dog Cappy. *jamesdietz.com*

Kelly Kennedy/Editor

KELLY KENNEDY IS THE managing editor for The War Horse. Kelly is a bestselling author and award-winning journalist who served in the U.S. Army from 1987 to 1993, including tours in the Middle East during Desert Storm, and in Mogadishu, Somalia. She has worked as a health policy reporter for USA TODAY, spent five years covering military health at Military Times, and is the author of *They Fought for Each Other: The Triumph and Tragedy of the Hardest Hit Unit in Iraq*, and the co-author of *Fight Like a Girl: The Truth About How Female Marines are Trained*, with Kate Germano. As a journalist, she was embedded in both Iraq and Afghanistan. She is the only U.S. female journalist to both serve in combat and cover it as a civilian journalist, and she is the first female president of Military Reporters and Editors. *kellykennedy.net*

Frank Sesno/Foreword

FRANK SESNO IS AN Emmy Award-winning journalist, educator and author whose broadcast career includes two decades at CNN as White House correspondent, anchor, Sunday talk show host, and Washington Bureau Chief. Sesno currently serves as the Director of Strategic Initiatives at the George Washington University's School of Media and Public Affairs and founder/director of Planet Forward. He is the author of *Ask More: The Power of Questions to Open Doors, Uncover Solutions, and Spark Change*. *franksesno.com*